ROOTS OF BLACK MUSIC

The Vocal, Instrumental, and Dance Heritage of Africa and Black America

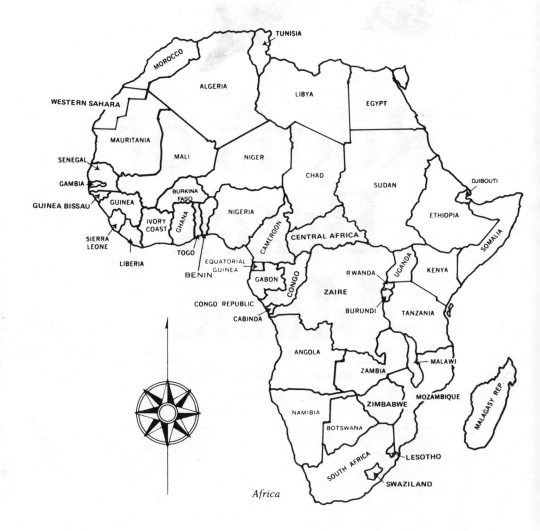

Africa

Roots of Black Music

The Vocal, Instrumental, and Dance Heritage of Africa and Black America

Ashenafi Kebede
Professor of Music

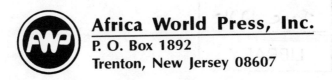

Africa World Press, Inc.
P. O. Box 1892
Trenton, New Jersey 08607

Africa World Press, Inc.
P. O Box 1892
Trenton, NJ 08607

Copyright © 1995, Ashenafi Kebede
First Africa World Press Edition, 1995

First Printing by Prentice-Hall, Inc., 1982
Second Printing by Ethius Books, 1989

Cover Design by Linda Nickens

ISBN 0-86543-284-8 cloth
ISBN 0-86543-285-6 paper

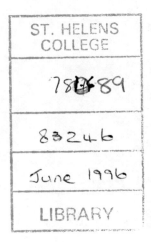

For Roberta, Nina, Senait, and Yared _____

Contents

Foreword

The proper business of ethnomusicology is precisely what Dr. Kebede has set out to do in this volume, to elucidate the lifestyle of a community through its music. The community he has chosen is nothing less than the homeland of black culture, Africa in all its multicultural complexity, and, by extension, certain of the lifestyles and musics that have grown up among blacks in North America. This ambitious task begins with vocal musics. Devoting a chapter to each area, the author discusses "oriental" Africa (the Islamic cultures of the north), the Nile cultures of the northeast, surviving traces of the pre-Islamic elements of North Africa, and Madagascar with its Southeast Asian influences. Dr. Kebede points out how these regions of Africa are often neglected by scholars of black music, many of whom consider that Black Africa begins south of the Sahara. He mentions the centuries-long flow of influences both ways between these regions and West, Central, and South Africa. The three latter areas are also introduced with a chapter each on their vocal music.

The voice is highly important in African music, and there have developed on the continent many varieties of styles of vocal production, from the tight, highly ornamented *melisma* of the Islamic North to the mellifluous yodeling, often on only two or three notes, of the Pygmies and Bushmen of Central and South Africa.

However, it is as instrumentalists that Africans are most widely known to the rest of the world. Particularly below the Sahara, Africa is that region of the world, more than any other, where the voice accompanies instruments rather than vice versa. Almost anything that resonates can be pressed into musical service in Africa. The inventory of musical instruments is breathtaking, as are the dazzling melodic and rhythmic uses to which they have been put. Dr. Kebede uses the basic rubric of the Mahillon-Sachs-Hornbostel instrumental taxonomy—idiophones, membranophones, aerophones, and chordophones—to introduce us to the musical instruments of Africa and then devotes a section of this book to the literary and religiophilosophic place these instruments have in African life. Chapter 12 of this comprehensive volume goes on to the consideration of dance, an inseparable part of the music.

The population of Africa is increasingly moving to the cities. The new lifestyles evolving there are reflected in a whole series of new musics, influenced by European and American instruments and musical genres and informed at every turn by African inventiveness. The influence of the mass media of communication, of feedback from the black cultures of the Diaspora, and the emergence of a "third stream" of composers of art musics, producing cantatas, masses, symphonies, and other "classic" forms, are considered in Part IV. An especially valuable contribution is the section of biographical sketches of such internationally known composers as Akin Euba, Fela Sowande, J.H. Kwabena Nketia, and Halim El-Dabh, who have arisen in Africa and have struggled to make themselves heard as the inevitable stream of influence and counterinfluence has taken place.

The book is unusual in its confrontation of the many sides of the question of the preservation of traditional musics. The author points out how "progress," the ubiquity of the mass media, and the exciting development of new musical ideas all seem to pose a threat to the continuation of traditional forms, heretofore considered uniquely "African." Should and can these be preserved? It is one of the most absorbing questions in the present-day musical world, and the reader is made to realize that it has no easy answers.

Part V deals specifically with the black music of the northern half of the Western Hemisphere, a subject that involves the history of North American music as a whole. The author presents a brief sketch of the development of blues and jazz from field calls and other African origins as well as from the influences of Euro-American musical forms and instruments. Chapter 17 contains biographical sketches of some of the most outstanding of the black musicians of North America.

The principal challenge in Dr. Kebede's book is how to approach such a broad canvas and still write a text accessible to students and laymen. The author does not write down to his audience. The vocabulary of Western music theory and the many musical terms in languages from all over Africa have to be used, and they are introduced with the skill of the practiced educator. Much of the coverage is necessarily brief—otherwise there would have been topics that could not have been introduced at all—but Dr. Kebede goes beyond the limitations of many introductory texts by treating certain areas of his own special expertise in considerable depth.

The advantage of having a book written on black music by an African can be seen throughout the text in many subtle ways and comes to one's attention with particular force in the discussions of African aesthetics and the comments on the treatment of African musics by non-African scholars. The detail on Fellasha chants and Ethiopian liturgical music and the lengthy description of the construction, tuning, and use of the *krar* are of special interest. Here we have the benefit of Dr. Kebede's own life experience. He grew up in Ethiopia, has taught music there, and founded the National School of Music, which has since produced most of Ethiopia's young music scholars, composers, and performers. At the same time, his many years of experience in the United States as student, teacher, and administrator have given him the perspective needed to communicate readily with students here.

The author, then, is an unusual man who in this book has done an unusual service to our understanding of music. In an introductory text of modest pretensions he has nevertheless provided a much-needed point of view, unusually broad coverage, and, in certain areas, extensive treatment of special interest. It is a text both scholarly and humane, both African and American.

David P. McAllester
Professor of Anthropology and Music
Wesleyan University,
Middletown, Connecticut

Preface

The creation of this book was preceded by several years of lesson planning while teaching graduate and undergraduate courses in ethnomusicology and black studies at the National School of Music, Ethiopia; Queens College; the Ph.D. program in music of the graduate school, City University of New York; Brandeis University; and currently at Florida State University. Hence, it is a result of several successful experiments in the classroom during a span of fifteen years. The continuous discussion of the purposes, goals, and means of black music studies with my students and colleagues was followed by a critical analysis of the results as I have observed them. The consequent urgent need for a new approach to the teaching of an introductory course in the music of African and African-derived peoples led to the development of the materials in this book.

Flexibility and Readability

Roots of Black Music is specially designed to be of value to the student or layman interested in gaining an understanding of music in the context of African and Afro-American cultures. Unlike most other books so far printed on African music, this work deals with both oriental and sub-Saharan cultures. Trade relations between northern and sub-Saharan Africans were maintained from ancient to present times. Merchants crossed the desert in both directions to sell and buy gold, salt, ivory, and cloth. Because the great majority of the people are Moslems, Islam is the unifying lifestyle in North Africa. The majority of the inhabitants are racially Mediterranean (caucasoids) with negroid admixture—including the Berbers and the Tuaregs (who are often classified as Berbers); the eastern Mediterraneans include the Egyptians, the Beja of Sudan in the Red Sea area, and most Ethiopians—such as the Amhara, Eritrea, Tigré, Galla, Somali, and Bu Nukimas. Consequently, racial classifications become rather complex and unnecessary. The most negroid tribes of sub-Saharan Africa have members with light skins, pale eyes, and caucasian features that are commonly associated with nonnegroid peoples. On the other hand, there are among the most causcasoid groups people with negroid features, such as averted lips, frizzy hair, and large flat noses. Hence, I have made every effort not to divide the peoples of the continent upon unclear racial lines (as almost all books have done in the past).

Organization

The term lifestyle is used to designate a distinctive manner or way of existence. In discussions of music, the term *style* alone operates at different levels of specificity. For example, we can be very general and speak of non-European or non-Western music style as opposed to a European or Western style of music. We can talk about an African music style, as distinct from the general non-Western music style. Similarly, we can also deal with a style of music that is black American. We can be specific and discuss the Nigerian style distinct from the African style of music. It is possible to be more specific and describe the minstrel *(azmari)* music style of Ethiopia; we can even specialize and discuss the style of a single performer within the *azmari* tradition. It is possible to describe the jazz style of music, as distinct from the general black American style of music. Still more specifically, we can describe the style of a single vocalist, such as Leadbelly. Description of a musical style includes its technical and artistic elements, methods of performance, the relationship of the performer(s) and the audience, attitudes toward music, the social role of the music, and its relationship with other branches of art such as dance, poetry, and drama.

The materials of the book are presented in five parts. The first deals with vocal music. Part II is devoted to the study of musical instruments. The mythological and symbolic attributes of music are presented in Part III. Dance is discussed in Part IV. Part V is concerned with urban music and the African roots of black American music.

All the sections on music contain carefully prepared discographies. These lists of recordings will provide the reader with a wide spectrum of musical examples especially chosen for their high degree of authenticity. This book is not just a compilation of secondary sources. It is also based on my own research, travels, and fieldwork in Africa, the Near East, and the United States of America. I have, however, consulted the works of numerous authorities on music in African and Afro-American cultures. Thus, the selected bibliography at the end of each chapter will serve as an excellent source of reference for those people interested in pursuing their studies on a subject at a more advanced level.

Acknowledgments

My colleagues Professors Paul Berliner, William Hughes, and William Kennedy were kind enough to read sections of the manuscript in rough draft. Professors Dale Olsen, David P. McAllester, and Caldwell Titcomb were extraordinarily generous with their time in reading the manuscript. They all provided valuable suggestions and have earned my deep gratitude. I am particularly grateful to Professor David P. McAllester, my teacher and friend, a great scholar, and a pioneer in the founding of the Society of Ethnomusicology, who kindly contributed the Foreword. Nina Ashenafi provided moral support and also helped proofread the galleys. My appreciation goes to copy editor Bruce Emmer, Prentice-Hall production editor Rita Young, and especially to Spectrum Books acquisitions editor Mary Kennan for their interest and hard work on the production of my work. This book is dedicated to my friend Roberta Recht, my son Yared Ashenafi, and to my two wonderful daughters, Nina and Senait Ashenafi, whom I love very much, and who have always been supportive and encouraging.

Credits

Francis Bebey, *African Music*, p. 38. (Copyright © 1975 by Lawrence Hill & Company, New York.) Reprinted by permission of the publishers.

Paul Berliner, *The Soul of Mbira*, pp. 25, 33, and 56. (Copyright 1978.) Used by permission of the University of California Press.

Paul Berliner, *The Soul of Mbira*, p. 55. Diagram: The Tuning Plan of Mbira Dza Vadzimu. (Copyright 1978.) Used by permission of University of California Press.

John Blacking, *How Musical Is Man?*, p. 51. (Copyright 1973.) Used by permission of the University of Washington Press.

Sir E. A. Wallis Budge, *A History of Ethiopia*, p. 8. (Copyright 1966 by Oosterhout N.B., The Netherlands.) Used by permission of Anthropological Publications.

Harold Courlander, *Negro Folk Music U.S.A.*, pp. 90, 136, and 137. (Copyright 1963.) Reprinted by permission of the Columbia University Press.

William R. Ferris Jr., "Racial Repertoires Among Blues Performers" in *Ethnomusicology* 14(3):443. (Copyright 1970 by *Ethnomusicology*.) Reprinted by permission of the Society of Ethnomusicology.

H. Macaulay Fitzgibbon, *The Story of the Flute*, p. 4. (Copyright 1914 Charles Scribner & 1929 William Reeves, London.) Reprinted by permission of William Reeves, London, and Charles Scribner's Sons, New York.

Theodore C. Grame, "Music in the Jma al-Fna of Marrakesh" in *The Musical Quarterly*, LXI(1):75. (Copyright 1970 by G. Schirmer, Inc.) Used by permission of the editor/publisher.

Tom Johnson, "Encounters with Griots" in *The Village Voice*, July 9, 1979, p. 58. (Copyright © 1979 by *The Village Voice*.) Reprinted by permission.

Thomas F. Johnston, "The Cultural Role of Tsonga Beer-drink Music" in *Year Book of the International Folk Music Council* 5:139. Music example and song-text. (Copyright 1973.) Reprinted by permission of the author and the International Folk Music Council.

Thomas F. Johnston, "The Cultural Role of Tsonga Beer-drink Music" in *Year Book of the International Folk Music Council* 5:132. (Copyright 1973.) Reprinted by permission.

Robert Kauffman, "Aesthetics and Shona Music" in *Ethnomusicology* 13(3):507–511. (Copyright © 1969 by *Ethnomusicology*.) Reprinted by permission of the Society of Ethnomusicology.

Ashenafi Kebede, "African Music in the Western Hemisphere" in *African Music*, pp. 131–136. (Copyright 1972 by UNESCO, Paris.) Used by permission of La Revue Musicale/UNESCO.

Ashenafi Kebede, "The Bowl-Lyre of Northeast Africa. Krar: The Devil's Instrument" in *Ethnomusicology* 21(3):379–395. (Copyright 1977 by *Ethnomusicology*.) Parts reprinted by permission of the Society of Ethnomusicology.

Ashenafi Kebede, "The Sacred Chant of Ethiopian Monotheistic Churches: Music in Black Jewish and Christian Communities" in *The Black Perspective in Music*, 8(1):21–34. (Copyright 1980.) Used by permission of the editor/publisher.

Ashenafi Kebede, "The Bowl-Lyre of Northeast Africa" in *Ethnomusicology* 21(3):390. Music example. (Copyright 1977.) Used by permission of the Society of Ethnomusicology.

Ashenafi Kebede, "The Sacred Chant of Ethiopian Monotheistic Churches" in *The Black Perspective in Music* 8(1):21–34. Notational signs and symbols. (Copyright 1980.) Used by permission of the editor/publisher.

Joseph Machlis, *The Enjoyment of Music*, p. 7. (Copyright 1977.) Used by permission of W.W. Norton & Company, Inc.

I VOCAL MUSIC

1 Song: Its Types, Functions, and Methods of Performance

The voice is the most natural, artistic, and spontaneous way of making music by means of the human body. Consequently, singing is the commonest and the most universal characteristic of all the music languages of the world's people. There is no society in the world that does not have vocal music.

Words and melody are combined in a *song*. Sometimes *vocables*, or linguistically meaningless syllables, are used to accompany a melody. Some songs consist of a repetitive, simple, and relatively short melody set to a long, complex, and continuous text or poem. A song in which a great poem is combined with an equally great melody enhances an artistic feeling in the appreciative listener. Songs, however, vary from culture to culture in their content, purpose, structure, form, text, aesthetics, perform-

ance, and many other socially defined traits. After all, music, like language, is culturally patterned sound. As there are many languages, so there are also many musics. Imagination and active listening will be required in order to understand and appreciate a few of the diverse musical languages of non-European cultures. A good listener is always an informed one. Cultural information and technical knowledge advance a better understanding of the feeling and significance conveyed by the sound of music. Active listening requires discipline and involvement. "Art, like love," Joseph Machlis has said, "is easier to experience than define."[1] The greater our knowledge and involvement, the higher our awareness and the intensity of our experience.

[1]Joseph Machlis, *The Enjoyment of Music*, p. 7.

3

Functions and Types of Songs

Music provides an excellent means for the presentation of words. This is another universal characteristic of music. Throughout the world's cultures, stories, plays, religious psalms and incantations, and emotional outpourings of all types are often presented through music.

Vocal music may be divided into two large categories: *sacred* and *secular songs*. *Sacred songs* in general serve the objectives of religious worship; the human voice is thus used as a medium of communication with the supernatural, with a god or gods, to enhance religious meditation or to advance peace and harmony between a person and his universe. *Chanting*, a recitation of religious texts, is used to appease spirits or deities in both monotheistic and polytheistic religions of the world.

We discover here probably the most important of all the functions of music: a person's constant search or desire for communication with the unknown, the supernatural, or a supreme being through the use of sacred chants and songs.

Secular songs are worldly by the intent and content of their texts. Love songs are the most common of the secular type. Secular song topics generally deal with all human experiences outside the sphere of religion. There are hunting songs, ballads, drinking songs, insult songs, and bawdy songs. Other secular song types express complaint or social commentary. These songs are concerned with interrelationships between the sexes, the social and political classes, and the individual and the family.

Musical experiences permeate the whole course of human life. Music in Africa and Asia, as in all non-European cultures, is deeply ingrained in the way of life. Thus, songs are performed when a baby is born or given its name or put to sleep. Circumcision songs are popular among people who practice it. Songs are used to educate the young. Some songs teach youth the male and female codes and mores of society; others are sung to correct unruly behavior. West Africans even claim to have songs that attract termites.

Some songs have both secular and sacred characteristics. In West Africa, for example, funerals are accompanied by vocal music and dance. These songs are sung to appease the spirit of the deceased in order to maintain harmony for the living; the dead body is lavishly entertained before it enters its final rest. The difference between sacred and secular is not always easy to define.

Styles of Performance

A song may be sung *solo*, by one person, accompanied or unaccompanied by an instrument. It is a common practice around the world to find a singer accompanying himself on an instrument; sometimes the same person may be the poet, composer, and performer. A solo voice may be accompanied by a single instrument or a group of instruments; in this case, the vocal melody is considered more important than the accompanying instrument(s).

A song may also be performed by two people, as a *duet*, or by three, as a *trio*. A *quartet* refers to a performance of music by four; *quintet*, by five; *sextet*, by six; *septet*, by seven; *octet*, by eight; the performance of music by nine persons is called *nonet*. The performers may be made up of any combination of vocalists and/or instrumentalists. A *chorus*, however, is an exclusive organization of more than nine singers. Most African and Asian vocal groups number between ten and twenty-five. Religious music is often performed *a cappella*, without instrumental accompaniment.

Texts of songs are generally set to melodies in two ways. The syllables of the text are equally distributed among the tones of the melody in a *syllabic song;* in other words, each syllable is sung to a tone. When one syllable is extended over several notes of the accompanying melody, the style of performance becomes *melismatic*. An example of a syllabic song is provided in Figure 1.1.

The versatility of the human voice is interestingly demonstrated in the areas of *voice masking* and imitation of musical instruments. Voice masking is often accomplished by singing or talking through a musical instrument, such as a horn or a flute. In this case, the instru-

Figure 1.1. A syllabic Amhara lullaby, "Ushururu."[2] *Text translation:*
Ushururu *(vocable) my child, my baby.*
1. *You are on my back when I grind and when I spin,*
   come down my baby, my back is sore.
2. *I, the baby's mother, will come back to see him.*
   Mother will bring him bread and milk in her arms.
   Ushururu, *my child, shururu.*

[2]For a version of this and many other lullabies, see Dorothy Berliner Commins, *Lullabies of the World.*

ment is used primarily as a megaphone, and the identity of the person singing will not be recognized by his voice. Wearing masks and voice masking are very common practices, particularly in the magicoreligious ceremonials throughout sub-Saharan Africa. The human voice can also imitate the sounds of nature—bird calls, mating calls of animals—as well as musical instruments. *Ululation*, a shrill, high sound, is often produced by women in oriental Africa to demonstrate pleasure over a performance or activity; it is used in many ways to express approval, similar to the Euro-American clapping of hands.

Song Structure

The performer communicates ideas to his listeners through music. Purely instrumental music, because of its illusive and intangible nature, may be harder to comprehend than vocal music. Meaning in vocal music is often direct, as long as the text sung is constructed to convey ideas and it is directly integrated with the melody. Sometimes melodies are primarily used to convey the message of the text; in this case, the text is considered more important than the melodies. This applies to the vocal music of oriental Africa. *Vocables* are also set to melodies, in which case the melodies are considered more important than the text. Pygmy vocal music has numerous songs that serve as excellent examples of this usage of vocables.

A *melody* communicates meaning because its constituent tones are patterned with significant relationships. We perceive as a unity the succession of tones in a melody. Some melodies are narrow in range; they may be made of only two or three tones. Other melody types may consist of many tones and have ranges of two or more octaves. Every tone of a melody has four basic characteristics: *pitch*, its highness or lowness; *duration*, a life span or the length of time it is sounded; *volume*, its loudness or softness; and *timbre*, its quality of tone.

The tones of a melody move in various directions to form a curve or line. Consequently, we describe melodies, according to their curve, as *ascending, descending, undulating,* and other combinations. *Motion* is another characteristic of a melody; the tones of a melody may be performed in close *stepwise motion*, or in skips and leaps, or a combination of both. *Range* refers to the distance from the lowest to the highest tone of a melody. *Tempo* refers to the rate of speed. As in a spoken language, some melodies consist of smaller units, such as sequences and phrases. Most melodies have a beginning, a middle, and an end.

A song may consist of only one repetitive melody. Another song type may consist of two or many varied melodies. Some songs have repetitive texts set to changing melodies, and vice versa.

When the same melody is repeated with every stanza, or strophe, of the poem, the song structure is in the *strophic form.* The *strophic song* is often performed solo, with or without an accompaniment. Sometimes slight variations exist between the verse lines. In other words, the verse lines are not exactly identical. Changing text lines are also set to standard repetitive melodic lines. Short instrumental *interludes* or bridges are popularly used to connect strophes in accompanied songs. Long solo interludes are used to bridge the wide gaps between song cycles. A cycle consists of a group of strophic lines that are rendered meaningfully. Although cycles of four strophes are popular, variations occur in different cultures as well as within song types. The strophic form is widely exploited in cultures where itinerant poet-musicians exist. Consequently, this directly applies to the esawa and gnawa traditions of Tunisia and Morocco the azmari tradition of Ethiopia, and the griot brotherhood of Sudan.

The *responsorial style* of singing is popular in most sub-Saharan cultures of Africa. The style is called responsorial when two musicians perform a song as if answering one another, or in a call-and-response manner. The simplest kind of response is performed by two persons; the second singer directly imitates or duplicates the part of the first singer; this is called simple or *imitational response.* The organization of performers varies depending on circumstances, individual or audience preference, type of song, and other social considerations. The responsorial approach commonly includes the part of a single leader and a group response.

When two groups of musicians perform in call-and-response, the style is *antiphonal.* The simplest form of antiphony includes two performers in each group. More than two large choruses performing independent, often overlapping parts, answering each other, and each chorus singing polyphonically, or in multipart, often creates a complex form and texture.

Briefly, and simply speaking, *texture* refers to the layers of sound heard at once in a music performance. There are three basic types of texture: *monophony*, which literally means "one sound," refers to music with a single melodic line; the *polyphonic* ("many-sounding") texture consists of two or more independent melodic lines performed simultaneously; and the *homophonic* ("same-sounding") texture consists of one main melody and supportive accompaniment which is used to enhance and strengthen the melody. Textures also shift from one to another kind in a musical performance; this is not, however, a common occurrence.

In closing this section on vocal music, we will classify song relationships into the following nine categories:

1. *Solo:* one singer

2. *Alternating solos:* two or more soloists

3. *Social unison:* all the singers singing the same text and melody throughout the song

4. *Responsorial:* leader-chorus alternation

5. *Antiphonal:* chorus-chorus alternation

6. *Overlapping response:* leader-chorus overlapping alternation

7. *Overlapping antiphony:* chorus-chorus overlapping alternation

8. *Hocket:* interlocking; two or more groups rhythmically distinct and melodically complementary

Basic Terms

If you aren't sure what each of the following terms means, look back at the text, where they appear in italic type. Additional information about some of them may also be found by checking the index.

song	ascending
vocables	descending
sacred songs	undulating
secular songs	motion
chanting	stepwise motion
solo	range
duet	tempo
trio	strophic form
quartet	strophic song
quintet	interludes
sextet	responsorial style
septet	imitational response
octet	antiphonal
nonet	texture
chorus	monophony
a capella	polyphonic
syllabic song	homophonic
melismatic	alternating solos
voice masking	social unison
ululation	overlapping
melody	response
pitch	overlapping
duration	antiphony
volume	hocket
timbre	

Bibliography

COMMINS, DOROTHY BERLINER, *Lullabies of the World*. New York: Random House, 1967.

MACHLIS, JOSEPH, *The Enjoyment of Music*. New York: W.W. Norton & Co., 1970.

NKETIA, J.H. KWABENA, *The Music of Africa*. New York: W.W. Norton & Co., 1974.

SACHS, CURT, *The Rise of Music in the Ancient World, East & West*. New York: W.W. Norton & Co., 1944.

Discography

African Story-Songs. Told and sung by Dumisani Abraham Maraire. University of Washington Press (1969). UMP-901.

Ba-Benzele Pygmies. (Recordings and commentary by Simkha Arom.) UNESCO Collection. BM 30 L 2303.

The Fiery Drums of Africa: Songs and Dances of West Africa. Dinizulu and His Africans. Eurotone 124.

Mbira Music of Rhodesia. Performed by Dumisani Abraham Maraire. Notes by D.A. Maraire and Robert Kauffman. University of Washington Press. UMP-1001 (Secular music.)

The Music of the Dan. Recordings and notes by Hugo Zemp. UNESCO Collection. BM 30 L 2301. (Winner of the Grand Prix International du Disque 1966, Académie Charles Cros, and the Preis der Deutschen Schallplatten Kritik, awarded by Fono Forum. For hocketing and intricate multipart vocal music by several performers, play bands 4 and 11.)

The Music of Ehtiopia: Azmari Music of the Amharas. Recordings and notes by Ashenafi Kebede. In cooperation with the Society of Ethnomusicology. Anthology Records AST-6000.

Voices of Africa: High-Life and Other Popular Music by Saka Acquaye and His African Ensemble. Edited by Kenneth S. Goldstein and Saka Acquaye. Nonesuch H-72026.

Wolof Music of Senegal and Gambia. Folkways 4462.

2 Vocal Music in Maghrib and Oriental Africa

In our context, the term *orient* refers to the societies of the Near and Middle East, both *inside* and *outside* the African continent, that share common cultural characteristics. The oriental African cultural zone mainly includes (1) North Africa—Morocco, Algeria, Tunisia, Libya, and Egypt; (2) the northern part of Mauretania and Sudan; (3) many societies in the northeast, the "horn," of Africa, which is largely occupied by Ethiopia and Somalia; and (4) the culture of the island of Madagascar. The geographical configuration and general physical features of these regions in relation to the countries of the Middle East and Asia are among the most important factors in the creation, formation, and advancement of the style of music known as *oriental*. It consists of a blend of African and non-African musical styles nurtured in the African soil by African peoples for many generations. These styles of music must be studied in the context of African cultures.

North Africa

The reason for the commonly held but erroneous view that North Africa, or *Maghrib*, is a place very much apart from the rest of the continent is clearly explained by Grame in the following manner:

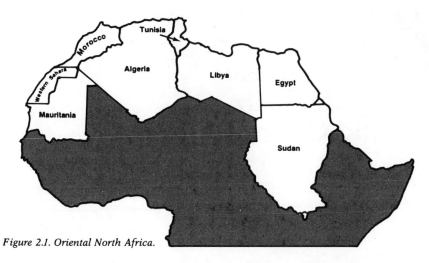

Figure 2.1. Oriental North Africa.

The reason for this lies in our belief that the Maghrib is a thin finger of "Arabic" or "Islamic" culture that extends from Egypt to the Atlantic; therefore, it is reasoned, it must be treated as a special case, and not brought into the mainstream of African studies. In other words, our attention is firmly fixed on an East-West cultural axis to the near exclusion of the North-South one.[1]

Evidence of the oldest monarchy in human history, dating back as far as 3300 B.C., has been discovered recently in Nubia of northern Sudan.[2] There are even indications that the Egyptian culture may have borrowed its advanced political and artistic organizations from this ancient Ta-Seti Nubian kingdom. The dating is based on correlations of artistic styles in pottery, incense burners, and other artifacts recovered from the Nubian Qusful cemetery with similar styles found in predynastic Egyptian artifacts that are relatively known and well

dated. It is also recognized that these Nubians used a system of writing. Descendants of the Ta-Seti royalty established the Sudanese kingdom of Kush which, in fact, gained a short period of sovereignty over Egypt.

Usually no mention is made of Egypt in studies that deal with Africa. It is, however, important to realize that Egypt, an African nation, was one of the most important centers of world civilization and exerted a decisive influence on the cultures of both the Occident and the Orient. Egyptian ideas in the fields of astronomy, acoustics, and music spread along with Egyptian conquests. The Egyptians were one of the earliest societies to establish a system of writing, around 3000 B.C. (others were China and Sumeria). Egyptians were also one of the first to experiment with a system of musical notation; the development of music as a profession in ancient Egypt is significant in the study of African cultures in general. Schools of music were established that trained not only vocal and instrumental performance, but also the-

[1]Theodore C. Grame, "Music in the Jma al-Fna of Marrakesh," p. 75
[2]*The New York Times*, March 1, 1979.

10

ory and *chironomy*—the art of notation by means of gesture. Obviously, the Egyptian influence on the Mediterranean cultures of Europe, Africa, and Asia was immense. As Malm correctly puts it:

> The Egyptians of Plato's time were still possessors of coveted knowledge in both music practice and theory. Thus, much that we credit to Pythagoras and other great Greek music theorists may have deeper roots in Alexandria and the Nile Valley.[3]

European theorists, composers, historians, and researchers have always been fascinated by the entire Egyptian culture, in its diverse branches, as a source of knowledge and inspiration. Even Napoleon Bonaparte sent a group of scholars to investigate every aspect of Egypt; one of them, G.A. Villoteau, a musicologist, undertook fieldwork and studied Egyptian music in Egypt from 1798 to 1800. His extensive account, published in French in the twenty-four volume *Description de l'Egypte*, is still used as a reference work and is especially important for its detailed description of the musical instruments. Sound recording devices were, of course, not yet available during Villoteau's time; hence, much of his work remains generally useless. Though this music did not leave material remains, like some of the other arts, the walls of Egyptian tombs and monuments chronicle important information about the music, musical instruments, and performance practices. Sometimes interesting song texts are found. Here is a translation of an ancient and famous Egyptian funeral song:

Let music and song be before you. Leave behind all evil and think only of joy until the day comes when we journey to that land that loves silence.[4]

Influences never operate in one direction only. The Egyptian heritage has also been bombarded with alien influences. Egyptians assimilated musical conceptions, performance practices, and musical instruments from neighboring African, Mediterranean, and Asiatic cultures with whom they came in contact. Over the centuries, the music and instruments of ancient Egypt have undergone drastic transformations. The numerous paintings on walls and inside tombs that have survived to this day depict a sophisticated musical heritage in ancient Egypt different from what we find today.

The most remarkable external influence comes after the advent of Islam, a relatively recent religious movement that dates back to the teachings of its founder Muhammed (A.D. 571–632). With the Islamic invasion of North Africa in the seventh century, Muslim cultural practices took firm root and flourished in Egypt. Thus, many of the instruments of the Islamic world are popularly used in the performance of modern Egyptian music. It is not at all surprising that Egypt is today one of the four major sites of modern Muslim classical music, the others being Iran, Tunisia, and Turkey.

The first Muslim invasion of Tunisia occurred in A.D. 668. The original inhabitants of this country, the Berbers, were converted to Islam or driven out of their native land. Today the largest Berber population is found in Morocco, where the traditional forms of their music have

---

[3]William P. Malm, *Music Cultures of the Pacific, the Near East, and Asia*, 2nd ed. pp. 82–83.

[4]*Ibid.*, p. 83.

flourished. By A.D. 713, Muslim armies had not only established themselves in most of North Africa, but had invaded and conquered most of Spain.

The Muslim states in Spain were known as Al-Andalus. "Andalusia" once referred to the highly sophisticated Muslim culture that flourished in Spain. Music became very important in the kingdoms of Al-Andalus, and musicians received patronage. Hispano-Arabic elements were blended in the *Andalusian school* of music. This school produced famous musicians who were able to transmit a high caliber of artistic performance to the later generations that fled to live in North Africa. Religion has always served as the most important unifying factor in the Muslim tradition; so the Muslims of North Africa have always maintained close cultural ties with Al-Andalus. In fact, when at last the Christian *reconquista* of Spain took over the Andalusian cities from the thirteenth century until the end of the sixteenth century, the Muslim inhabitants gradually fled to North Africa. These refugees in Tunisia, Morocco, and Algeria maintained and cultivated the Moorish-Andalusian musical style. Today *Andalusian music* refers to the classical music that flourished in North Africa, particularly in Tunisia and Morocco.

The Styles of Music

Most of pan-Islamic folk music is vocal. Usually the adjective "folk" is mistakenly used to identify the peasant culture in rural areas; city dwellers are not considered "folk." Obviously, this is a wrong interpretation and usage of the term. "Folk" here refers to any group of people who share something in common, such as music, dance, religion, language, and so on. City dwellers also have their own folk music. Hence we speak of pan-Islamic folk music in three categories: traditional music, classical music, and contemporary or urban music. There are also different types in each category. Defining these terms is consequently very difficult. The following descriptions are intended to serve as a general guide.

Traditional music is ordinarily performed by the common people, not by the professionally trained musicians; its repertory consists of material that has been passed down through the generations by means of oral tradition, by word of mouth. Caravan songs of the desert nomads and wedding songs are examples of traditional music.

The term *classical* refers to the genre of music and musical performance that has been developed and advanced by specialized schools of music, transmitted to, and performed by, generations of professional musicians; much of the Andalusian music of North Africa is an excellent representative of this category. Most of the classical songs consist of long poems composed by known poet-musicians. The subject matter is often love, as is the case with a song type called *ghazal* or *zajal*. It is important to note that the classical Andalusian style of music is most developed in Tunisia and Morocco.

Popular or *contemporary music* refers to urban music; it is also described as neotraditional or acculturated music. It blends both interethnic and international styles, and is found in all urban localities of contemporary societies. Taverns and night clubs often foster the development of urban music. Technology and the communications media, especially radio, have greatly accelerated cross-influences between nations and advanced change in music. The influence of European music is pronounced in this category of contemporary music.

In Morocco, a great part of the traditional music is often performed by hereditary minstrels or craftsmen called *gnawa* and *esawa* in most of oriental Africa, including Morocco and Tunisia. (They are known as *gewel*, meaning "griots," among the Wolof people of Gambia.) All these bards sing *qasida* songs of praise to Muhammed and other Islamic saints. They are professional entertainers; they sing stories *(halam)*, accompanying themselves on stringed instruments. Most musicians belong to a guild, a religious brotherhood, or an association in order to protect or advance their mutual interests. In this case, both *gnawa* and *esawa* belong to religious fraternities; both adhere to the Muslim faith. Both the negroid *gnawa* and the less negroid *esawa* also integrate dance, poetry, and singing in most of their performances.

Historically, the forefathers of the black *gnawa* came as slaves to Morocco from West Africa; their music exhibits many important characteristics that are similar to their ancestral home. In addition to their large repertory of song and dance on diversified topics, they are well known for their healing ceremonials and snake-charming rituals. Women do not participate in the healing ceremonials. The snake-charming ritual includes the participation of about five of these itinerant minstrels as well as the spectators. Women accompany the sung prayers on a *bandir* (frame-drum), while the men handle the serpents. The oboelike *ghaita* (shawm) is considered an important musical instrument in this ritual.

Observe here how the roles of women change from function to function following social prescriptions. In one function, the snake-charming ritual, they play an important role; in another function, the healing ceremonial, they are completely excluded. Also note that both the healing ceremonial and the snake-charming rituals are a hybrid of quasi-religious and quasi-secular activities; consequently, they do not fit the secular-sacred antithesis of European classification. This holds true for many of the productions found in most of the African musical cultures.

Music—vocal or instrumental, sacred or secular—is often performed in *monophony*, without harmony, or in group *heterophony*, pseudo-unison. Vocal music always takes precedence over instrumental music. In fact, oriental African cultures manifest a high degree of sophistication and artistic vitality in the sphere of vocalization, poetry, and versification. *Zajal* is an important oriental African vocal form found in Tunisia, which uses classical poetry set to music. *Fondu*, which means "the best diamond," consists of secular songs that use texts in the idiomatic language of the common people. These song types are all chanted by a chorus.[5]

The Andalusian *nuba* may be considered one of the most important classical genres of North African music. It consists of a series of sections or movements. Usually, a *nuba* starts with an improvised instrumental introduction or prelude in an unmeasured rhythm. Unlike the first section, the second includes rhythmic instruments and is performed by an ensemble in very slow tempo. The third section consists of an unornamented chant, whereas the fourth section is an instrumental interlude in a fast-moving duple meter. A virtuoso performer usually plays the fifth section solo. The sixth section is a joyous ornamented chant in a lively triple meter. The last section, the finale, is very fast and lively, performed with great fervor, as it is the climax of the *nuba*. Although this is the general stylistic scheme of most *nubas*, variations also exist.

The Muwashshah Form

Muwashshah ("encircling") is a strophic form of vocal music performed in North Africa and the Arab Near East. It belongs to Islamic art music. Performed by a chorus or by a chorus alternating with soloist, *muwashshah* is often accompanied by a few musical instruments. The musical material is based on a repetitive *iqa*, or rhythmic mode, and *maqam*, or melodic mode.

Although many varieties exist, the structure of the *muwashshah* may be generally divided into three sections. It is important to remember that none of these sections is more climactic or important than another; all Islamic art forms, including music, are nondevelopmental. Note also that all the sections end with the same refrain (A₁), as follows:

    Section I: *Dawr* ("cycle")
    A The opening strophe
    A₁ Refrain

[5]UNESCO Collection recording *Tunisia*, with commentary by Alain Daniélou.

    Section II: *Khanah* ("inn")
    B New Musical material
    A₁ Refrain
    Section III: *Qaflah* ("closing")
    C New poetic material, often accompanied by melody A
    A₁ Refrain

The composers of *muwashshah* are known. One of the well-known Egyptian poet-composers, Ibn Sana'al Mulk (1156–1212), wrote a book, *Dar al Tiras*, that explains the techniques of composing it; he also included many of his own works as examples. Today *muwashshahat* (plural) are popularly performed and heard, live and through the media, in Egypt as well as in the other countries of North Africa.

In the performance of *muwashshahat* compositions, narration and mood portrayal are completely avoided; unlike European art forms, there is no musical "painting." The texture is always monophonic. Dynamic variations are also avoided.

The text is neither narrative nor dramatic; the theme often includes descriptions of nature, courage, lamentation, and patriotism. Most of the love songs consist of double meanings and are sung in a platonic manner; the love of God dominates the topic. All these characteristics give the *muwashshah* an abstract quality according to the Islamic art form.

Music in the Sudan

The Sudan covers an unusually vast area. It borders on eight countries, including Egypt and Ethiopia; the Nile River passes through these three countries. As the result of continuous migration, the Sudan is the home of numerous independent ethnic groups. Today northern Sudan is principally populated by four major ethnic groups: the *Nubians, Mahass, Shaigia,* and *Galien.* These people live around and near the Nile River valleys.

Vocal music is highly developed among the inhabitants of northern Sudan. The Nubians and Mahass speak and sing in a language called Nubian; the Shaigia and Galien use Arabic.[6] Their large repertory of music includes satirical, love, wedding, and epic songs. There are also elegies, sacred praises to the Prophet and Muslim saints. Specialized songs exclusively sung by men and others sung only by women are popular. Preference is given to textual rather than melodic content; consequently, new or varied stanzas are sung to standard melodic lines—a performance preference commonly practiced in most oriental African cultures. The instruments used to accompany vocal music include bowl-lyre types, similar to the Ethiopian *krar,* the *al-kaita* (shawm, also known as *ghaita* in Morocco and Tunisia), and a variety of small drums. The *al-kaita* is at times performed solo and is associated with a dance called the *zihee.* The three-holed *zumbara* flute often accompanies *dobeit,* a song type popularly sung by the nomadic Galien during their long night journeys.

Patriotic song and dance types are widely performed by the nomadic peoples of western Sudan, particularly in the provinces of Kordufan and Darfur. Satirical songs, or *gardage,* are sung solo by a woman, often accompanied by an *umkiki* (fiddle). Usually these female vocalists have earned community respect for their ability in versification and improvisation; they are also known to be scornful of their enemies. Numerous wrestling songs, a wealth of dances and songs performed as part of initiation rites for boys, and *kambala,* sung stories of heroic deeds, are abundantly found in this area. Rattles of all kinds—those worn on the leg, ankle, or wrist and those types shaken by hand—accompany many of these songs and dances.

Songs and dances of possession and exorcism are distinctive features of east-

[6]Mahi Ismail, "Les Traditions musicales du Soudan" [Musical Traditions in the Sudan], *La Revue Musicale,* pp. 87–93.

ern Sudan. One well-known type is *moshembe-da*, a ritual performed to exorcise evil spirits. A couples dance and song commences the *moshembe-da*. It is followed by the dance of the *kujour*, the Sudanese shaman. The smoke of burning herbs, spices, and coffee beans marks the presence of the evil spirit. The *kujor's* dance ritual is gradually accelerated to a frenzy by the rhythmic instrumental accompaniment; the instruments often include one *bangia* (lyre) and four two-holed *penah*, wind instruments of varying sizes made of gourds. Each *penah* produces only two or three notes. The four *penah* are played staccato or detached in *hocket*, a process of interlocking melodic fragments, in order to provide a markedly rhythmic accompaniment to the dance. The exorcism of the evil spirit is symbolized by inhalation of the smoke and exit of the *kujour* from the house. This is the culmination of the *moshembe-da* ritual. Many of the performance styles found in eastern and southern Sudan consist of traits that are a hybrid of both oriental and sub-Saharan cultures.

Non-Islamic Indigenous Music of Oriental African Cultures

Historians have exaggerated the "Arabic" and "Islamic" influence on African music to the point of distortion. Arabia has existed only since 300 B.C. According to the Tunisian historian Ibn Khaldin (1332–1406), music as an art was completely unknown to the Arabs of pre-Islamic times. However, one should be skeptical of such a sweeping statement.

Islam did not begin until the seventh century, during the lifetime of Muhammed (571–632). Islamic culture refers to the way of life popularized by Muslims. The Islamic attitude toward music and musicians has always been negative. While no specific law against music is found in the Koran, the Hadith, a book of stories about and sayings of Muhammed, depicts the Prophet as looking on it with disfavor. Even today this negative attitude toward music and musicians survives in most of the Islamic cultures of the world because the political, religious, and economic dominance of Islam over most of oriental Africa is great.

There also exists an indigenous and truly African style of music, cutting across oriental Africa from north to south and east to west, that is not influenced by the Arabs. The Egyptian civilization was the cradle of music. Even the Greeks referred to Egypt as the source of their musicopedagogic ideas. Nearly 2500 years ago, before Arabia was known, Herodotus commented on the Egyptian achievement in the following manner:

> ...there is no country that possesses so many wonders, nor any that has such a number of works which defy description.[7]

The authentic characteristics of ancient Egyptian music are still preserved in the

[7]E.A. Wallis Budge, *A History of Ethiopia*, pp. 1–8.

performance practices of the Coptic churches. There is also no doubt that the Egyptian influence is deeply rooted in what is erroneously characterized as "Arabic." The people of Arabia were relatively backward during the glorious days of the Axumite civilization at the Horn of Africa. Court and religious vocal music were highly developed, and as part of the noble heritage, every member of the aristocracy received educational training in the art of versification and vocalization. The ancient African practices of the Axumites are today preserved and presented in the Amhara music of Ethiopia.[8]

Another pre-Islamic African style is found in Berber music of North Africa. The kingdom of the Berbers, the native inhabitants of North Africa, covered a vast expanse of territory stretching from North to West Africa in prehistoric times. It housed the dominant culture of pre-Islamic North Africa. Gradually driven out of their land into the mountains by the introduction of Islam, Arabic migrations, and invasions, the Berbers still preserve their ancient heritage. Unlike the Muslims around them, they practice monogamy and other indigenous culture traits that are particularly Berber. The Berber style, Grame writes,

> has nothing whatever to do with "Arab" influence; but probably represents an ancient African style. It has always astonished me that the "scholarly" community is resolutely unaware of the existence of a style of African music that seems to cut across the continent from roughly Ethiopia to the Atlas mountains.[9]

Systematic analysis of cultural trends from prehistoric times to the present points to the existence of an indigenous musical style in many parts of oriental Africa.

Music in the Malagasy Republic

Another interesting style of music is found in the dominant and oldest culture of the African island of Madagascar, now officially known as the Malagasy Republic. It blends Malayo-Polynesian and African characteristics and, as its name implies, it exhibits remarkable influences especially from Malaya. The migration of people from Southeast Asia to, and their settlement in Madagascar has been confirmed by historians; the current cultural practices are also living testimonials. The main language spoken by the Madagascan belongs to the Malayo-Polynesian family, although it also draws on dialects of the original African peoples there.

The intercultural admixture is so far-reaching that it extends to the Islamic and European spheres as well. In the area of musical performance, for example, the famous open-air theatricals known as *hira-gasy* employ a large repertory of long moral songs that are accompanied by a variety of instruments, including tube and box zithers *(valiha)*

[8]Ashenafi Kebede, *The Music of Ethiopia*, pp. 29–39.

[9]Personal communications with T.C. Grame.

reminiscent of similar Indonesian zithers, along with Islamic-type fiddles *(rebab)*, French-type drums, and African Chopi-styles xylophones. The vocal music often uses scales and harmony that are clearly derived from the sub-Saharan musical zone, especially in the use of parallel thirds.

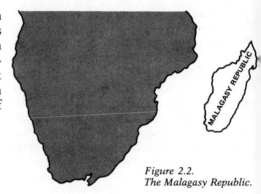

Figure 2.2.
The Malagasy Republic.

Basic Terms

If you aren't sure what each of the following terms means, look back at the text, where they appear in italic type. Additional information about some of them may also be found by checking the index.

oriental	muwashshah
chironomy	iqa
Andalusian music	maqam
traditional music	krar
classical	al-kaita
ghazal	zihee
zajal	zumbara
contemporary music	dobeit
gnawa	gardage
esawa	umkiki
gewel	kambala
qasida	moshembe-da
halam	kujour
bandir	bangia
ghaita	penah
monophony	hocket
heterophony	hira-gasy
zajal	valiha

fondu	rebab
nuba	

Bibliography

BUDGE, SIR E.A. WALLIS, *A History of Ethiopia*, vols. I & II. London: Oxford University Press, 1928.

AL-FARUQI, LOIS IBSEN, "*Muwashshah:* A Vocal Form in Islamic Culture," *Ethnomusicology* 19 (1, 1975):1–29.

GRAME, THEODORE C., "Music in the Jma al-Fna of Marrakesh," *The Musical Quarterly* LXI (1, 1970):74–87.

KEBEDE, ASHENAFI, *The Music of Ethiopia: Its Development and Cultural Setting.* Ph.D. dissertation, Wesleyan University (Middletown, Connecticut), 1971. "Non-Western Music," in Roger Kamien, *Music: An Appreciation.* New York: McGraw-Hill Book Co., 1976, pp. 514–39.

ISMAIL, MAHI, "Les Traditions musicales du Soudan" [Musical Traditions in the Sudan], *La Revue Musicale* (UNESCO, Paris) 288–289 (1972):87–93.

MALM, WILLIAM P., *Music Cultures of the Pacific, the Near East, and Asia.* 2nd ed. Englewood Cliffs, New Jersey: Prentice-Hall, 1967, pp. 82–83.

Discography

Algeria (Sahara). Recordings, commentary, and photographs by Pierre Augier. UNESCO Collection Musical Atlas. EMI-Odeon 3C 064-18079.

Arab Music (Music of the Near East). Lyrichord LLST 7186.

Morocco I: The Music of Islam and Sufism. Recordings and notes by Philip D. Schuyler. UNESCO Collection. BM 30 SL2027.

Music of Morocco. Recorded by Christopher Wanklyn. Ethnic Folkways Library FE 4339.

Musique Berbère du Haut-Atlas. Recorded by B. Lortat-Jacob and G. Rouget. Collection Musée de l'Homme. Vogue LD 786.

Musique Maure. Republique Islamic de Mauritanie. Recordings by Charles Duvelle. Ocora. OCR-28.

Sudan: The Music and Song of Abdel Karem el Kably. Afro-Tone (International Record Industries).

Taqasim and Layali: Cairo Tradition. Recordings by Jacques Cloarec. UNESCO Collection. Philips 6586-010.

Tunisia. Recordings and commentary by Alain Daniélou. UNESCO Collection: A Musical Anthology of the Orient. BM 30 L 2008.

3
Northeastern Africa: The Nile River Cultures

It is safe to say that no sacred topics known to the western world have been so persistently discussed, argued about, studied, and widely documented as Christianity and Judaism. It is not only their history, teachings, and influences that have been investigated on a worldwide basis, but also the role of music in Jewish and Christian worship that has been the occupation of many outstanding minds in countless numbers of books. There is one, and only one, area in the world that has been bypassed in these investigations and even today remains outside, and that is Ethiopia. The scholarly community still knows little about the Ethiopian branches of Judaism and Christianity—their origin, teachings, and forms of worship. Even less is known about the sacred chants of these two important religions in Africa.

First, Ethiopian isolationism has kept the country apart from the rest of

the world. With the exception of two comparatively short periods—the first three hundred years of Ethiopian Christendom (ca. 330–650), a period of extensive international activity, and the reign of Empress Zewditu and Haile Selassie I (1917–1974)—the world forgot about Ethiopia, by whom it in turn was forgotten. "Encompassed on all sides by the enemies of their religion,"[1] Ethiopia remains to this day an African island of black Jews and Christians.

Second, the number of foreign scholars sufficiently familiar with the Ethiopian languages, music, and other branches of culture to be able to investigate these areas is almost zero. During the centuries of isolation, and at all other times, Ethiopian scholars *(debterawoch)* and chroniclers kept historical records, both in handwritten manuscripts and

[1]Ashenafi Kebede, "The Sacred Chant of Ethiopian Monotheistic Churches," p. 21.

20

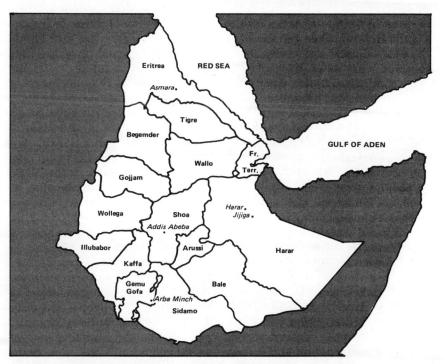

Figure 3.1. Ethiopia.

later in the format of printed books. Most of these documents, chronicles, and manuscripts were written in *Ge'ez*, the ecclesiastic language, and *Amharic*, the common secular language. These languages, with their script and large vocabulary, have proved to be too difficult for foreigners to master within a reasonable period of time for purposes of understanding and translating Ethiopian books into other languages.

Third, the proud Ethiopian personality has contributed to the discouragement of foreign students who wished to investigate Ethiopian culture. Ethiopians in general have always been distrustful and suspicious of foreigners. The upper-class nobility and the knowledgeable priests especially have been reluc-

tant to share information with Europeans, who often acted arrogantly and introduced themselves as "Ethiopic scholars before their first lesson on Ethiopia."[2] Ethiopia practiced a form of Judaism long before the Christian era; Ethiopia accepted Christianity when most of Europe was pagan. "Who are these Europeans to tell us that our forms of Judaism and Christianity are more primitive than theirs? And why?" Ethiopians ask. Even members of other African countries and most African-derived peoples erroneously believe that Judaism and Christianity are religions of the white European world.

The *Kibre Negest* (or Glory of Kings), one of the most important historical

[2]*Ibid.*, p. 22.

21

books written in *Ge'ez,* elaborates on the exodus of the Hebrews from Jerusalem to the Ethiopian Empire at Axum about two thousand years ago.* It clearly explains the conditions under which the Ark of the Covenant was brought to Ethiopia and how Judaic practices, including chanting, started; and this information is supported by the Gospels. It reveals that Ethiopia believed in one God around 1000 B.C. The numerous migrations of Semitic peoples from South Arabia to north and northeastern Africa during that time has been attested to in books as well as by cultural remains and artifacts.

The *Fellasha* are the so-called "black Jews" of Ethiopia who practice a form of orthodox Judaism. The *Fellasha,* however, call themselves *ye'izrael lijoch,* "the children of Israel," and *beta izrael,* "house of Israel"; they claim to be not only ethnically Jews but direct descendants of those Israelite nobles and priests who came to Ethiopia accompanying Menelik I, the alleged son of King Solomon and the Queen of Sheba. As their ancestors were men who intermarried with the native African women in Ethiopia, the Fellasha consider themselves Afro-Semitics. The Fellasha oral tradition regarding their Hebraic origin and their present musical practices appears to be reasonably accurate. There is, in addition, a solid historical foundation for these traditions.

As ethnomusicological documentation and serious study of Fellasha chant has great significance not only for an

understanding of music in the context of Ethiopian culture but also for the comparative study and understanding of sacred chant, intercultural influences, and uses of music in religious worship in the context of Hebraic and Christian cultures around the world. The Fellasha tradition certainly consists of the oldest Jewish chant in the world. Powne correctly states, "While most Christian chant presumably has its roots in Jewish practice, Ethiopian chant probably has a closer relationship than most."[3] Musicologist Gustave Reese detected ethnic links between "Ethiopian psalmody as sung today" and Hebrew chant.[4]

The Fellashas are found today mainly in regions north of Lake Tana. They live congregated in large close-knit communities in Uzeba and Seqelt. Although their culture is rapidly disappearing and their number getting small as they gradually get absorbed by the larger Ethiopian population, Fellasha are still found in small villages scattered around the northern Ethiopian provinces of Begemdre, Semyen, and Tigré.

The present cultural practices of the Fellasha clearly demonstrate many striking elements of Judaism. The synagogue, for example, is the most important and the central part of the village life. The Sabbath, Saturday, is celebrated with strict reverence, according to the Jewish faith. The Fellasha festivals include the New Year (Rosh Hashana), the Day of Atonement (Yom Kippur), the Feast of the Tabernacles (Sukkoth), and Passover (Pesach). The Fellasha are highly particular about their food; they do not eat dishes prepared by a non-Fellasha or animals that are not permitted by the

---

*The Ethiopic text of the *Kibre Negest* was published by Bezold with a German translation (Munick, 1905); an English translation was published by Budge (London, 1922). This most important reference work was compiled by Ethiopian chroniclers to prove the ethnic links between Ethiopian and Hebrew patriarchs.

[3]Michael Powne, *Ethiopian Music.*
[4]Gustave Reese, *Music in the Middle Ages,* p. 93.

Old Testament. Vocal music, particularly chanting, plays an important role in all phases of their culture.

Furthermore, among the Fellasha of Ethiopia, male children are circumcised on the eighth day after birth. Similar ceremonies are observed among all the Afro-Jewish communities of Tunisia, Morocco, and many other thinly populated areas of northern Africa. These ceremonies are accompanied by chanting. Song is also important as part of the other Afro-Jewish festivals, such as the aforementioned New Year, Day of Atonement, and Feast of the Tabernacles.

Fellasha Chant

The origin of the Fellasha chant, as the Fellasha themselves, remains shrouded in legends and stories. We will discuss, however, a few of its outstanding characteristics as it is performed today in Fellasha communities. Perhaps it may even be possible in the future to construct a relatively objective cultural history from the chant. Fellasha chant is almost entirely vocal music. On a few occasions, however, such as the celebration of the New Year, it is accompanied by sistrums, drums, and bells. Stone chimes are also used, but not to accompany chanting. They mark time and call members of the community to prayer meetings.

Prior to the Muslim invasion of northern Ethiopia in 1892, when Muslim bandits destroyed monasteries and burned their religious books, the Fellasha conducted services in Hebrew. Today they speak and chant in *Ge'ez*. In the recitation of sacred texts, an admixture of syllabic and melismatic styles of chanting are employed. Each syllable is clearly enunciated; long melismas are sung vibrato, with a throbbing and nasal vocal quality. Ornamentation, including

Figure 3.2. Ethiopian Saint Yared singing before Emperor Gebre Meskel (top). Ethiopian priests chanting and dancing, accompanied by drums (bottom). Both from a traditional color painting. All rights reserved, Ashenafi Kebede Collection.

Figure 3.3. Fellasha chant.

the placement of eliding and sliding mi- crotonal inflections, is used before or after the main syllabic tones. Vocables are rarely used. Accurate intonation always is considered important. When performing as a group, the Fellasha chant heterophonically, or in pseudo-unison. The chanting progresses in recognizable melodic phrases or formulas memorized by the cantor(s). The temporal aspect of the chant is completely governed by the text. Therefore, it is often sung in free-rhythmed, or *parlando rubato*, style.[5] The Fellasha divide their chanted prayers into ten types according to the times or

[5]Listen to *Ethiopia: The Falasha and Adjuran Tribe* side one, and *Ethiopia: Vol. I, Music of the Central Highlands*, side one, band 4.

24

sa'at of performance. These are sunrise, forenoon, midday, afternoon, before sunset, sunset, bedtime, midnight, before dawn, and dawn.

Here is one good musical example of a Fellasha syllabic recitation.[6] The text translates as follows:

Lord, I cry out to you, hear me.
When I call to you, my God, hear me.
I cry out to you, hear me and save me.
When I call to you, when I pray to you, you visit us from heaven, from your prepared dwelling place. Hear my voice.
Lord, I heard your voice, and I was frightened...[7]

The Christian Church in Africa

A second event of vital importance was the introduction of Christianity in Africa. Historical and Biblical accounts attest to the fact that one of the Three Wise Men who visited the new-born Christ child laden with gifts was an Ethiopian prince. It is obvious that Christian practices are not exclusively European in origin. On the contrary, most Europeans were still practicing paganism when Ethiopia accepted Christianity as a state religion around A.D. 333.[8] It was Ezana, the king of Axum and a member of the Solomonian line of Ethiopian monarchs, who formally introduced the new religion into the country.* Prior to his conversion to Christianity, he believed in *Igzi-abher*, One Perfect God, equivalent to the Biblical *Yahweh;* it is most likely that he was a Fellasha. Ethiopian sources indicate that he converted to Christianity in order to gain major political advantages around the Mediterranean and Red Sea zones through achieving "Christian brotherhood" with the then powerful Roman Empire. The members of the nobility and high clergy received Christian baptism following in the lead of their monarch. Consequently, Christianity was superimposed over the existing Fellasha forms of Judaism and religious chanting.

This point—the superimposition of Christianity over Judaic practices in Ethiopia—has to be clearly understood, because it provides us with a background and framework for a discussion of the beginning and development of monotheistic practices *prior to* and *after* the rise of Christianity. Comparatively speaking, there are many similarities between the Fellasha Temple and the Christian Church:

1. The shape and construction of the church, in one case, the temple, in the other, are similar. Both are round.
2. In both cases, the priests are all men. Women play no part in religious services.

*Under the leadership of Judith Gudit, a Fellasha woman revolutionary, the black Jews, known in history as the Zagwe dynasty, took away the throne from the Axumite Christians around the middle of the tenth century; eleven Zagwe kings ruled after Judith for over three hundred years at their new capital, called Lasta. For additional information, see E.A. Wallis Budge, *A History of Ethiopia*, pp. 213–216.

[6]Kay Kaufman Shelemay, "Historical Ethnomusicology," p. 257.
[7]*Ibid.* Collection of, and transcribed by, K.K. Shelemay.
[8]See E.A. Wallis Budge, *A History of Ethiopia*, p. 148.

3. In both cases, chanting was intended and used as the sole expression of the belief in one God. It is almost entirely sung; it is the human voice, not a musical instrument, that is considered important.
4. In both cases, the religious leaders and active participants are divided into three groups: deacons, priests, and scholar-educators.
5. In both cases, the congregation does not take part in singing.
6. In both cases, *Ge'ez* is used as the sacred language.[9]

The Christian churches and monasteries, however, received patronage from the monarchs and became centers of learning and artistic activity. Ethiopia committed her Christian liturgy to writing at the beginning of the fifth century. Except in Egypt, there were no systems of writing used to record liturgy before this time; the question of external influence is not applicable here. It is also very impor-

tant to note here that Ethiopians alone among the people of the African continent have had a written script for nearly two thousand years.[10]

Under Christianity, the translation of the Holy Scriptures and other literary works of antiquity was completed. Monasteries and the imperial court with their *scriptoria* were the workshops in which beautifully illuminated manuscripts were produced.[11] These manuscripts were produced on parchment *birana*, a durable and time-resisting material which has enabled us to know and admire the masterpieces produced many centuries ago. The monastic system was also a powerful agency in the development, creation, and preservation of culture. It gave birth to a system of formal church education that educated music, poetry, gesture, and personality development. A system of notation was introduced as part of the Church's objectives to preserve its large repertory of sacred chants.[12]

The System of Notation

Jewish cantillation uses a system of notation that is similar to the Ethiopian system. Within the Orthodox Christian Churches, Syrian, Armenian, and Egyptian manuscripts between the seventh and twelfth centuries show the use of notational symbols, signs, and letters. The Egyptian notation is no longer in use today; it has become a strictly oral tradition. The Syrian and the Armenian

churches use a notational system that is simpler than the Ethiopian. Only the Jewish and the Ethiopian systems have survived to this day. However, a great deal of work remains to be done in order to explain their precise relationships. We can indicate at this point, however, that the Ethiopian notation "is the most de-

[10]*Ibid.*

[11]Ashenafi Kebede, *The Music of Ethiopia,* pp. 34–52.

[9]See Ashenafi Kebede, "La musique sacrée de l'Eglise Orthodoxe de l'Ethiopie."

[12]See Kebede, "The Sacred Chant of Ethiopian Monotheistic Churches," p. 25.

veloped system, and extends to all the music of the church, not just to the cantillation of the lessons."[13]

Most Ethiopian authorities credit Yared with having invented Ethiopic notation. *Saint Yared*, the greatest of all Ethiopian scholar-musicians, lived during the reign of King Gebre Meskel (476–571).[14] But an Ethiopian manuscript, found recently in Paris, states that it was two nonecclesiastic learned men, Azaz Gera and Azaz Raguel, who introduced notation during the reign of Emperor Gelawdewos (1508–1540), obviously many years after the death of Yared.[15] Church personnel find this most unacceptable due to the fact that both Gera and Raguel were civilians devoid of divine knowledge and untrained in the practices of the Holy Church. To be sure, it is also possible that notation might have been introduced to the Ethiopian Church before Yared's time. History states that Frumentius, the first Ethiopian bishop, was a Phoenician. Phoenicians, who accomplished the change from syllabic to alphabetic writing around 1500 B.C., may have also made similar progress in the area of notation, at least around the beginning of the Christian era.[16] Phoenicians might have been invited by Frumentius to work within the Ethiopian Church, and they would have brought notation with them. Although this is all hypothetical, the possibility that notation may have entered Ethiopia before Yared's time is just as strong as the possibility that Azaz Gera and Raguel may have invented it. Yared

was given sainthood for the invention of the notation system among his other great contributions.[17]

Ethiopic notation employs both *milikitoch* neumatic signs (curves, dots, dashes, etc.) and *siraye* letter notation taken from the *Ge'ez* alphabet.* For purposes of easy identification, the *siraye* letter notation is often placed above, while the *milikit* or neumatic signs are placed below the text of the manuscripts. The *siraye* consists of small letters usually written in red ink; the *milikitoch* are easily recognizable by their distinct shapes, and they are often written in black ink. Although neither the signs nor the letters indicate individual pitches, they clearly remind the knowledgeable cantor of melodic passages, each with its own relative pitches; each passage is both melodically and textually meaningful. The duration of each pitch, silence, and volume is also measured according to their inportance within each passage and the entire chant as a whole.

The neumatic signs specifically indicate performance approaches, such as tempo, dynamics, and special ornamental inflections. In order to clarify their performance implications, I give the following list, which consists of the most important *milikitoch* with their *Ge'ez* names and their precise meanings in English; equivalent Italian musical terms are provided wherever possible.

Definite pitch values were never recognized in the church music. Modal and melodic phrases were known under the generic term *zema* (Hebrew and Ara-

---

[13]Michael Powne, *op. cit.* p. 95.

[14]Kebede, *Music of Ethiopia*, pp. 34–52.

[15]*Catalogue des MSS Ethiopiens de la Bibliothèque Nationale* (Paris, 1877, p. 76).

[16]See Kebede, *Music of Ethiopia*.

[17]*Ibid.*

*Syllabic, neumatic, and tablature notational systems exist in many Asian and oriental African cultures. In most cases, the notation has cosmological or religious connotations.

Notational signs of the Ethiopian Church music

1.	• ይዘት	*yizet*	Detached and accented tone. Derived from the verb *meyaz*, to hold. Equivalent to *staccato*.
2.	⌣ ደረት	*deret*	Sing in a low, deep voice. Chest register. Also applies to singing with the lips closed, with clenched teeth, and with deep chest resonance. Humming at the lowest range of the male voice.
3.	♩ ቁናት or አቅና	*Kinat* or *aKina*	Upward *glissando*. Both terms are derived from the verb *maKnat*, "to raise up."
4.	⌐ ሞረት	*Ciret*	Start high and proceed with downward *glissando*. The *Ciret* vocal melody is often connected to a cadence. The term is derived from *Cira*, "tail."
5.	⌒ ድፋት	*difat*	Drop the voice. Skip to a lower range. Often refers to singing an octave lower. The root erb is *medfat*, "to throw down."
6.	Ⱶ ቁርጥ	*KurT*	Refers to singing a cadential formula which often ends on the home tone. Its root is *meKureT*, "to end" or "to cut." Equivalent to *coda*.
7.	ᴧᴧ ሩጥ	*ruT*	Throbbing, warm, and expressive singing style with rapid but narrow pitch fluctuations. The term is derived from *meroT*, "to run." Equivalent to *vibrato*.
8.	⁖ ርክርክ	*rikrik*	Rapid repeat of a single syllabic tone. This style of singing usually creates a sense of tension at the high range. Equivalent to *tremolo*.
9.	↙ ሂደት	*hidet*	Gradually getting faster and louder. Sing each syllable distinctly. Equivalent to *accelerando*, *crescendo*, and *portamento* at the same time.
10.	╱ ሠረዝ	*serez*	Slight pause.

bic, *sama*), each *zema* or melodic phrase being phonetically indicated by a letter or a combination of letters. The letter notation consists of abbreviations of words in the sacred text; the syllables of each word are sung according to a style prescribed by ecclesiastic tradition. The difficulty in understanding the notation lies in the fact that it is impossible to study the melodic formulas represented by letters apart from the liturgy of which they are an integral part. Any attempt to study the liturgy would involve knowledge of *Ge'ez* and memorization of texts in numerous volumes of books. Even after all the memorization, the performance aspect of the chant, including expression, interpretation, and improvisation, is dependent upon each individual's skill and artistry, for there is no uniform interpretation of the notation or style of performance.

The Style of Performance

There are three technical *Ge'ez* terms that refer simultaneously to tonal range and performance principle, with the psychological implications of the chant to be performed. The terms are *ge'ez* (not to be confused with the name of the language), *izil*, and *araray*. In a wider reference, the terms refer to three octave ranges: low, middle, and high. *Ge'ez* means low, first or foundation, and free. *Izil* refers to the middle range, secondary, and moderate. And *araray* refers to high, ornamented, and fast chant. Sometimes these terms are used to refer to the starting tones of chants. In this case they serve a function parallel to the terms in the Vedic chant of the Hindus, where the lower note is *anudatta*, the middle tone *udatta*, and the high tone *svarita*.

Animation, elation, and outbursts of happiness and fulfillment are expressed in the high *araray* vocal range. Chants comemorating the birth of Christ are chanted, for example, in this *araray* range and in the *silt* mode. *Ge'ez*, on the other hand, has a low tonal range; it is sung in a relaxed, soft, and sad voice in a rhythm-free style. Feelings of despair, disappointment, and sorrow are expressed in this low range and in the *ge'ez*

yezema silt or *ge'ez* performance style. *Izil* is sung in the comfortable, ordinary, and medium vocal range. It is regarded as emotionally neutral, and that is why most of the chants of the Ethiopian Christian Church are performed in this performance style. Hymns of the ordinary days are performed in the *izil silt*. It should be emphasized here that tonal dimensions, such as low, middle, and high, do not have strict divisions; they are all relative. The different voices in a group performance may commence singing in diverse pitches, each person starting on a pitch appropriate for his voice; the result is heterophony or pseudo-unison.

Figure 3.4 is a sample transcription of music of the Ethiopian Church. It is sung by priests, though sometimes knowledgeable members of the congregation may join in the performance. Members of the priesthood also lead in the clapping. One priest beats on a two-faced *kebero* (drum).

The voices utilize a five-tone or pentatonic scale. Because of diversity and general lack of correspondence between Ethiopian singing and the European tempered sound system, the transcrip-

Terms used to indicate rates of speed		
መረግድ	*meregd*	Very slow, broad, and solemn. Equivalent to *largo* and *grave*.
ንዑሥ፡መረግድ	*nuis-meregd*	Slow. Literally "faster than *meregd*." Equivalent to *adagio*.
አቢይ፡ፀፋት	*abiy-tsefat*	Moderately fast. Equivalent to *allegretto*.
ፀፋት	*tsefat*	Fast. Equivalent to *allegro*.
አ ርዋፂ	*arwaSi*	As fast as possible. Equivalent to *prestissimo*.

Figure 3.4. Music of the Ethiopian Church.

MM 55

30

a - - - - ha-du - - - , wu - i - tu - -

- - - - , me - - - ni - - - -

- - fe - - - si - - - , ki-du - -

32

tion is an attempt to explain graphically to those familiar with staff notation some of the structural elements of the church's music; consequently, the transcription does not represent the music; it only serves a descriptive purpose. Note, however, the outstanding features of the music: the melody is highly melismatic; it consists of many ornamental subtleties, such as slurs (∿), vibratos,

upward (∿∿) and downward (∿∿) elisions and glides; note also how the drum maintains beats in a compound duple meter (⁶⁄₈) over the simple triple (¾) of the voice part; it is clear how those who clap take their cue from the drum. Listen to authentic sound examples of this music and attempt to incorporate the ideas and use the terms discussed in this chapter.

Basic Terms

If you aren't sure what each of the following terms means, look back at the text, where they appear in italic type. Additional information about some of them may also be found by checking the index.

debterawoch	difat
Ge'ez	KurT
Amharic	ruT
Kibre Negest	rikrik
Fellasha	hidet
ye'izrael lijoch	serez
beta izrael	zema
parlando rubato	sama
sa'at	izil
Igzi-abher	araray
Yahweh	anudatta
scriptoria	udatta
birana	svarita
Saint Yared	silt
milikitoch	ge'ez yezema slit
siraye	izil silt
milikit	meregd
yizet	nuis-meregd

deret	abiy-tsefat
Kinat	tsefat
aKina	arwaSi
Ciret	kebero

Bibliography

BUDGE, SIR E.A. WALLIS, *A History of Ethiopia*. The Netherlands: Anthropological Publications, 1966.

KEBEDE, ASHENAFI, *The Music of Ethiopia: Its Development and Cultural Setting*. Ann Arbor, Michigan: University Microfilms, 1971. "La Musique sacrée de l'Eglise Orthodoxe de l'Ethiopie" in *Ethiopie: Musique de l'Eglise Copte*. Berlin: International Institute for Comparative Music Studies and Documentation (IICMSD)

————, "The Sacred Chant of Ethiopian Monotheistic Churches: Music in Black Jewish and Christian Communities," *The Black Perspective in Music* 8(1—1980):20–34.

POWNE, MICHAEL, *Ethiopian Music: An Introduction*. London: Oxford University Press, 1968.

REESE, GUSTAVE, *Music in the Middle Ages*. New York: W.W. Norton & Co., 1940.

SHELEMAY, KAY KAUFMAN, "Historical Ethnomusicology," *Ethnomusicology* 24(2—1980):233–258.

Discography

Ethiopia: The Falasha and the Adjuran Tribe. Recordings and notes by Lin Lerner and Chet Wolner. Folkways FE 4355.

Ethiopie: Polyphonies des Dorze. Collection Musée de l'Homme. Le Chant du Monde LDX F74646. See Kebede's review in *Ethnomusicology* 23 (3—1979):481.

Music of the Cushitic Peoples of South-West Ethiopia. UNESCO Collection, Ethiopia I. Recordings and notes by Jean Jenkins. Barenreiter Musicaphon BM 30 L 2305. See Kebede's review of the above recordings in *The World of Music* XI (4—1969):70–73.

Music of the Ethiopian Coptic Church. UNESCO Collection, Ethiopia I. Recordings and notes by Jean Jenkins. Barenreiter Musicaphon BM 30 L 2304.

The Music of Ethiopia: Azmari Music of the Amharas. Recordings and notes by Ashenafi Kebede. Produced in cooperation with the Society of Ethnomusicology. Anthology AST 6000.

The Music of the Falashas. Recordings and notes by Wolf Leslau. Folkways FE 4442.

4

Vocal Music in Sub-Saharan Africa: The West and South

The term *sub-Sahara* refers to an enormous zone that includes practically all the cultures south of the Sahara Desert. Music forms an integral part of the societies' activities in this zone; thus, it is to be studied in the context of diverse traditions, as well as numerous genres of music within each tradition. According to the black African tradition, society is thought to consist of four general groups: (1) the gods and goddesses, (2) the ancestors, (3) the humans—living and recently dead, and (4) the natural world. Hence, music is closely associated with the various aspects of culture, such as poetry, religion, drama, magic, and dance. This applies especially to the cultures of West Africa, which consists of the peoples of Mauritania, Senegal, Gambia, Mali, Guinea, Sierra Leone, Liberia, Ivory Coast, Ghana, Upper Volta, Niger, Togo, Benin, Nigeria, and Cameroon. (It is this important West African region that has been called "Negro Africa," "Africa proper," or "Black Africa" and has been the topic of numerous studies, to the unfortunate exclusion of oriental Africa.) Southern African cultures include the peoples of the Republic of South Africa *(Azania)*, Southwest Africa *(Namibia)*, Zimbabwe, Lesotho, Swaziland, Botswana, Zambia, and Malawi. (South Africa is largely dominated by European settlers; consequently, it has numerous musical styles that are European-oriented as the result of cultural blending or acculturation.)

In most of sub-Saharan Africa, where rhythmic activity is considered to be the primary attribute of musical performance, the instrumentalists are required to possess an ability to sing well. In addition, musicians must have a good memory, exceptional fluency in their native languages, and familiarity with the oral literature and history of their re-

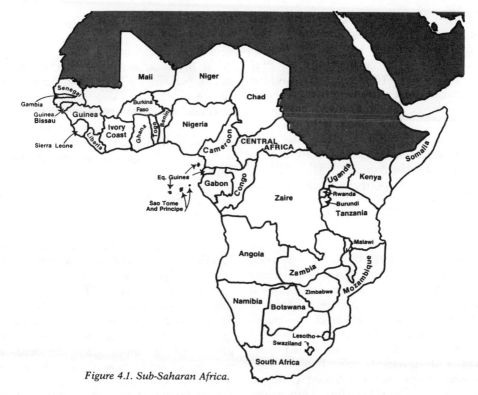

Figure 4.1. Sub-Saharan Africa.

spective traditions. This is notably true among the Gogo of Tanzania and Dagomba of Ghana—to mention only two of hundreds of traditions in Africa.

The African involvement in music begins before birth, when there is singing and dancing to ask the gods for a safe delivery. Then there is music to celebrate birth. There are even songs for name-bestowing. *Lullabies* are the first real melodies heard and appreciated by a newborn child. They are found all over the world because mother love is truly universal. Consequently, lullabies are love songs. The mother's presence is recognized by the baby through her tender voice; her singing means security, peace, and comfort. Lullabies may be sung with

or without words; although mothers often sing praises and promises, fairy tales and legends, infants are naturally too young to understand them. Primarily, these songs are used to lull an infant to sleep.[1]

Sometimes children are taught a song to sing, or have one sung to them by others, when they get their first tooth or when they lose one, as is the case among the Dahomey of western Africa. The child learns songs from his parents, other adults, and his peers. Among the Venda tribe of South Africa, there are children's songs called *nyimbo* that are sung in the

[1]Dorothy B. Commins, *Lullabies of the World*, pp. xi–xii.

37

daytime; there are the *ngano* songs that are sung in the evening and during the late fall and winter seasons. The Venda people have a large repertoire of *children's playsongs*. These songs are an integral part of the children's games.[2] A herdboy who carelessly allowed cattle to stray into another man's field may be punished by having to clean the field while singing a designated song repeatedly. Among the Ashanti of Ghana, children sing a song of insult at the habitual bedwetter.

Venda children also learn songs to express mockery or insult. A song may, for example, be sung to mock a boy who is considered a sissy or to tease women who are working hard. Great importance is put on counting songs, by which a child learns to count and name his fingers, toes, or other parts of the body. Sometimes these songs are used to "count out" or designate someone to perform a disagreeable job. It is chiefly through songs that the Venda children learn about their families, important people and events in their tribe, and norms of right and wrong.[3]

Passing from childhood into puberty is a momentous occasion in which songs play an indispensable role. Through songs, the facts of life, the roles men and women play in society, and the principles of family living and adult obligations are taught to the youngsters. Circumcision for boys and initiation ceremonies for girls employ song and dance.

Marriage is one of the most important occasions celebrated in a person's life. There are, according to most African traditions, three days considered most important in human life: a birthday, a wedding day, and a day of death. Consequently, the wedding day, no matter what the economic situation, is always accompanied by festivity, music, and dance. There exists a serious competition between the families of the groom and the bride as to which will provide the better wedding party and entertainments to go along with it. (The enormous expense involved in this affair has, in fact, led many parents into bankruptcy and at times has ended in broken homes.) Sometimes professional musicians are hired to sing and improvise poetry in honor of the groom and the bride. Worthy village dancers and singers are invited to perform in groups. Until the marriage is legalized officially, the two families—the groom's and the bride's—identify each other as the opposite camp. Hence, the texts are sung in praise of the groom at his camp, while the bride is praised in her camp. Witty but derogatory remarks are also exchanged between the members of the two families, each proudly claiming to be better than the other; some hostility even remains long after the wedding, until it is resolved by the birth of a baby to the married couple.

In a purely social setting, music also has an important role. Many African cultures have a large number of *drinking songs*, which are sung on occasions such as making arrangements for marriage, and celebrating a birth or a return from initiation school. Gifts of beer are sent; singing and dancing take place. The objective of the occasion is explained through songs.

Because of its great social significance, beer-drink music is popularly performed by the Tsonga of Mozambique and the northern Transvaal. It is used in

[2]John Blacking, *Venda Children's Songs.*
[3]*Ibid.*, p. 86.

the celebration of important life-cycle occasions "such as birth, dropping of the umbilical cord, closure of the fontanel, first walking, first menses, initiation, return from initiation, betrothal, marriage, pregnancy, death, and the various ongoing stages in the spirit-world."[4] The complete native text of the song in Figure 4.2, which we have not included here, is translated as follows:

the overlap between the call and response creates harmony. Descending pentatonic melodic patterns are often repeated to changing verse lines accompanied by handclapping, drums, or both.

Political songs serve as a means of learning the laws, customs, and political institutions as well as a means of expressing personal opinions about those in authority. Currently, many songs of this

Figure 4.2. *Tsonga beer-drink music.*[5]

Byala Hi Lebyi Maseve!
(Here is Beer!)
Transpos.: dim 5th up

♩ = 154
Cycle: 8

Call: Here's beer at the betrothal!
Response: In in-lawship!
Call: Sharing beer at the betrothal!
Improvised line: Hurry, hurry, I lack my share![6]

In most cases, performance of these songs uses an overlapping response; and

nature speak of independence or of protest. The following song text from Ethiopia is cited here as an example of social commentary:

> Ethiopia shall always
>   enthrall her enemies,
> Securely protected by her sons,
> From the scavenging western
>   wolves.[7]

[4]Thomas F. Johnston, "The Cultural Role of Tsonga Beer-drink Music," p. 132.

[5]*Ibid.*, p. 139. Collection of, and transcribed by, Thomas F. Johnston.

[6]*Ibid.*, p. 133.

[7]Many record jackets and journals contain English transliterations of song texts from several African languages and dialects.

Vocal music permeates the whole course of a person's life. There are song types that combine complaint and social commentary. They may be compared to the blues of Afro-Americans, though their contents and styles of performance may be different. These song types reveal a good deal of valid information pertaining to relationships between the sexes, the social and political classes, and the individual and his family. Merriam tells us that the performer may express deep-seated feelings not permissibly verbalized in other contexts.[8] This is, of course, one of the ways that members of the African and African-derived societies maintain a healthy state of mind.

Many cases are known where troubled people keep singing for days without eating in order to "sing away" all their woes. Yet in some areas, music must be constantly performed to *choreomaniacs*, people who are possessed by a compulsion to dance for a long time. The performance can be ended only when the choreomaniac stops dancing, and cases are known where men and women dance until they drop dead. Instances are found among tribes in Nigeria, Kenya, and Sudan, as well as in other non-African musical cultures.

Then there are *work songs*—particularly if the work requires repetitive physical movements, such as digging, felling trees, or chopping wood. A very interesting example of a case in which music itself does the work is found among the Feli of north Cameroon, who have a musical method of attracting termites to be used as food. A certain type of drumming and humming is performed

on top of open calabashes placed on the ground, producing a sound similar to that of rainfall. Deceived by the "rain," the termites come forth and are caught.[9]

In white-ruled South Africa, music serves as an emotional outlet for the enslaved black peoples. In fact, one black musician from that area summed up the importance of music in the following manner:

> They make new laws for us to obey, and we shall obey them; but if they tried to stop us from singing, then, I promise you, there would be a revolution in two days.[10]

In sub-Saharan Africa, music is integrated with the activities of society. Music is played in rituals concerned with warding off evil spirits. Most black African societies traditionally believe in polytheistic religions. Music, poetry, and dance are performed to celebrate the days of the various deities. Gods are appeased by sacrifices and songs. Wearing masks and reenacting life situations in the form of a drama, particularly in times of adversity, enhance peace and harmony. Native healers cure the sick by singing songs and performing prescribed dances. In Ghana, the priest-healer chants special *klamas* (memory aids) to the god of medicine to help in selecting a curative herb.[11]

The curative and therapeutic uses of music are gradually beginning to gain recognition outside Africa, particularly in the United States, where music is used in hypnosis, therapy, and psychiatry.

---

[8] Alan P. Merriam, *The Anthropology of Music*, p. 190.

[9] *Musique centrafricaine*. Recording and commentary by Charles Duvelle. Side two, band 4.

[10] *Ibid*. See record jacket notes.

[11] J.H.K. Nketia, *Folk Songs of Ghana*.

Basic Terms

If you aren't sure what each of the following terms means, look back at the text, where they appear in italic type. Additional information about some of them may also be found by checking the index.

Azania
Namibia
lullabies
nyimbo
ngano
children's playsongs

drinking songs
political songs
choreomaniacs
work songs
klamas

Bibliography

BLACKING, JOHN, "Trends in the Black Music of South Africa, 1959–1969," *Musics of Many Cultures*, ed. Elizabeth May. Los Angeles: University of California Press, 1980, pp. 195–216.

———, *Venda Children's Songs*. Johannesburg: Witwatersrand University Press, 1967.

COMMINS, DOROTHY BERLINER, *Lullabies of the World*. New York: Random House, 1967.

JOHNSTON, THOMAS F., "The Cultural Role of Tsonga Beer-drink Music," *Year Book of the International Folk Music Council*, vol. 5 (1973), pp. 132–155.

LADZEKPO, ALFRED K. and KOBLA, "Anlo Ewe Music in Anyako, Volta Region, Ghana," *Musics of Many Cultures, op. cit.*, pp. 216–231.

MENSHA, ATTA ANNAN, "Music South of the Sahara," *Music of Many Cultures, op. cit.*, pp. 172–194.

MERRIAM, ALAN P., *The Anthropology of Music.* Evanston, Illinois: Northwestern University Press, 1964.

NKETIA, J.H. KWABENA, *Folk Songs of Ghana.* Legon, Ghana: University of Ghana, 1963.

Discography

Africa East and West. Edited and narrated by Mantle Hood. Institute of Ethonomusicology, UCLA. IER 6751.

Africa South of the Sahara. Introduction and notes by Alan P. Merrian. Folkways FE 503.

East Africa: Bantu Music. The Columbia World Library of Folk and Primitive Music. Collected and edited by Alan Lomax. Vol. X, No. 91A 02017.

French Africa. The Columbia World Library of Folk and Primitive Music. Collected by Alan Lomax. Edited by Andre Schaeffner and Gilbert Rouget. Vol. II, No. 91A 02015.

Music of Tanzania. ILAM No. 25. GALP 1320.

Musique centrafricaine. Recordings and commentary by Charles Duvelle. Ocora OCR 43.

Sounds of Africa. Verve FTS 3021.

Venda Music. Recorded by John Blacking. University of Washington Press.

For additional sound examples, use the discography at the end of chapter 1. Most of the records with commentaries and notes contain song texts.

5 Vocal Music of Central Africa

Central Africa includes the Republics of the Congo (*Brazzaville*), Gabon, Central Africa, and Chad (these four independent countries were formerly known as French Equatorial Africa) and the western parts of Uganda, Zaire, Tanzania, Burundi, Rwanda, and the northern part of Angola.

The development of elaborate and polyphonic vocal melodies is widespread among the Pygmy peoples of central Africa.[1] Pygmies are classified into four groups, according to their spoken dialects: the Ba-Binga, Ba-Ngombe, Ba-Mbuti, and Ba-Benzele Pygmies. All Pygmies are nomadic hunters and gatherers with loose tribal organization. Pygmy groups exist in parts of Gabon, Zaire, and other central African countries where they are known by names given to them by the surrounding peoples; in these cases, the Pygmies adopt the languages of their neighbors.

These small Pygmy peoples of Africa live in the marshlands and forest areas of central Africa—areas usually feared and considered uninhabitable by the other neighboring tall tribes, such as the Watutsi. To the Pygmy, the forest is not dangerous. On the contrary, it is the source of all good; it provides food, shelter, peace, and protection; it is endowed with power. The Pygmies have a form of *monotheistic* religion. They believe in *Nzambi*, one God or Power that is naturally good. It is undoubtedly a complex form of religion. The forest symbolizes this all-powerful God. The Pygmies are also *monogamous*, each male marrying only one female at a time—unlike their western neighbors, who are generally *polygamous*, with many wives, and simultaneously *polytheistic*, believing in many gods. Their eastern neighbors, the Watutsi, have a few practices similar to

---

[1]See Rose Brandel's *The Music of Central Africa* and "Types of Melodic Movement in Central Africa."

the Pygmies; they are both monotheistic and monogamous. But unlike the Pygmy peoples, whose music is truly *polyphonic* and multipart, the warlike Watutsi use musical styles that are generally *monophonic*.

Multipart songs and dances are probably best developed among the Pygmies of all the peoples of Africa. Some of their performance styles remind us of contemporary European avant-garde music at its best. They possess a delicate balance and sense of harmony. A group performance technique known to us as *hocket*, an interlocking melodic fragmentation, is an important part of the Pygmy musical heritage. There are simple and compound types. In a *simple melodic hocket*, two voices alternate with one another at the same pitch level. *Compound melodic hocket* is identified by two or more voices alternating at different pitches. The yodel, a quick switch from chest to head voice, is a prominent vocal style among Pygmies. Glottal attacks, grunts, hums, and shouts combined with upward and downward releases are often employed. Pygmies have, in addition, melody types that are sung melismatically with trills and *tremolos*, repeated tones by rapid up-and-down vocal glides.[2]

Horizontal and vertical *hemiola* techniques—complex techniques that include variation and superimposition of diverse metric organizations—are an important part of the Pygmy performance tradition. Three groups of two beats are superimposed over two groups of three

beats in the most common type of hemiola.

Pygmy vocal music consists of five major genres: (1) songs that belong to the religious societies of men, known as *molino*, (2) songs sung by religious societies of women, or *elima* songs, (3) hunting songs, (4) gathering songs, and (5) play songs. Play songs include dancing, drinking, and bawdy songs. The Pygmy musical style is largely based on religious expression. Elephant hunting songs, for example, are performed with purpose and great seriousness. After all, the Pygmies use its meat for food and its skin for shields, shelter, and warmth. Songs are sung to appease the spirit of the elephant before and after the animal is killed; most of the activities that accompany hunting may thus be considered to be sacred.

Like most nomadic peoples of the world, Pygmies do not have instrumental music of their own, although some instruments are sometimes borrowed to accompany their songs and dances. Pygmies often perform on the instruments of their neighbors. For example, they often barter with the Bantus; they bring the products of the forest to Bantu villages to exchange them for coffee, sugar, spices, and other farm products. The Bantu people are by far the most numerous in Gabon and the surrounding area. Their original home was in eastern Nigeria, near Cameroon on the savanna and forest land. Their occupations included fishing, hunting, and farming. When Nigeria became overpopulated owing to migrations from the Sahara, the Bantu moved north to Sudan and later south to the Congo forest, Cameroon, and Gabon, where some of them mixed with the indigenous inhabitants, including the small Pygmies

[2]Listen to Pygmy and Pygmy-styled music on the following records: *Music of the Ba-Benzele Pygmies; Musique centrafricaine* (Play band 2 for Ba-Binga music); and *The Music of the Dan* (Play bands 4 and 11 for Pygmy-styled hocketing and intricate multipart vocal music by several performers).

and the larger black ethnic peoples. Bantu people of the Congo area are still skillful farmers scattered in kinship groups; they have built villages and towns as centers for the non-Bantu nomads around them. Today the Bantu are found even in South Africa. These non-Bantu nomads come to trade or intermarry. Pygmies are a good example of interethnic interaction through trade. The performance of music and dance is an important part of their activities.

Pygmies, widely regarded as great performers, always entertain their Bantu hosts when they are in a Bantu village. They sing and dance, accompanied by slit-gongs and drums, instruments made by their neighboring Bantus. Other instruments that accompany Pygmy dances and songs include the *lukembi* (also called *sanza*, *mbira*, and a host of other names here and there); idiochordic zither; the *mapili*, a board zither; the nose flute; and the musical bow. The inventive pygmies even use bottles, spoons, and sticks, along with non-African instruments such as the European guitar, in their performance of a few of their contemporary or acculturated songs. Their group dances demand very agile and acrobatic movements.

Extra-musical Connotations of Music and Musical Performance

A religious attitude toward music and musical performance is maintained by most of the societies of Central Africa. Sacred music especially is performed and preserved with a high degree of authenticity because it is based on magicoreligious expression. In other words, the practitioners safeguard it from change as much as possible in order to keep their art potent. The art of magical healing practiced by the *shaman* incorporates chanting and dancing in ceremonies that often last the whole night. The healing ceremonial is accompanied by special drums and rattles. The shaman, who belongs to the priest class, performs the art of magical healing for the sick as well as ensures the maintenance of health among the members of his immediate community.

Ceremonials include initiation rites. Male circumcision as well as female clitoridectomy are part of initiation; rebirth is the important theme. Adolescent boys are initiated into manhood through formalized ceremonies. Sometimes their initiation is symbolized by a change in outward appearance— they trim their long hair and dress themselves as men, following the dictates of the tribe. Totemism and animal imitation greatly enhance the initiation ceremonials. Totemistic musical instruments accompany the songs and dances; symbolism and sometimes even anthropomorphism are attributed to some of these instruments. The *bull-roarer*, with its weird ghostlike humming sound, is symbolic of the demon's presence. According to Bebey, the Dogon of Mali conceive the sound of the bull-roarer to be the voice of the ancestor who first encountered death.[3] Consequently, the sound symbolizes the presence of this remote ancestor as well as "the power of the ancestor whose death has been transmitted down from generation to generation." The friction drums, the pipes, the rattles, and other instruments are endowed with obvious sexual symbolism. In addition to ceremonial music, other types of songs appropriate for birth, marriage, death, hunting, seasons, entertainment, and the airing of grievances are found in Central African vocal music.

The importance placed on music and musical performance varies among the diverse African traditions; contrary to the generally held notion, music is not an ongoing day-to-day activity of all African peoples. For example, among the Amhara of Ethiopia, weeks pass without any kind of musical activity; when music is performed, it is commonly in the hands of the *azmari*, the professional musicians, who go directly to homes where family events such as weddings and births are being celebrated. Among the Basongye of West Africa, days pass without musical activity; Merriam has also observed among the Basongye that "there is but one event which occurs periodically over relatively short periods of time requiring music performance: at the first appearance of the new moon a ceremonial is practiced in connection with the village fertility figure and protector."[4] A third contrasting example is found among the inhabitants of the desert and forest areas; almost continuous musical activity takes place among the Pygmy of the Ituri Forest and among the *Bushmen.*

Bushmen inhabit the Kalahari Desert of southern Africa. Their rounded faces, pronounced cheekbones, and slanted eyes give them a rather Mongolian look. But unlike Mongolians, they are short, averaging under five feet. Though one of the oldest surviving groups in Africa, they are definitely neither black nor white; they are yellow-brown. (Their generic origin remains obscure.) Like the Pygmies, Bushmen are nomadic hunters and gatherers. They eat wild roots, berries, melons, honey, and other produce of the desert area; they hunt (with bows and poisoned arrows) rabbits, groundhogs, gnus, hartebeests, and other animals found in the desert. They have also, like the Pygmies, interacted culturally with the Bantus.

All members of the Bushman community participate in an ongoing musical performance. Some listen to solo and special group performances in a trance-like state, almost completely immersed in the music; active listening is a highly developed trait of the Bushmen. Most of their music is vocal. They do use a few musical instruments, including the linguaphone, *mbira*, and a one-stringed simple fiddle (made of bamboo, sinew string, and often a gourd resonator). There is a close relationship between the sound of their language and singing; tongue clicks, suction stops, explosive ends, throaty gurgles, and other sounds are used in both activities. Bushmen also talk, and sometimes sing, while inhaling and exhaling. These qualities of their vocal style of performance makes the music of the Bushmen among the most original and fascinating of the numerous traditions in Africa.

More information about the instrumental traditions of these regions is provided in Part II.

[3]Read Francis Bebey's *African Music*, p. 38.
[4]See Alan P. Merriam's *The Anthopology of Music*, p. 75.

Basic Terms

If you aren't sure what each of the following terms means, look back at the text, where they appear in italic type. Additional information about some of them may also be found by checking the index.

Brazzaville
monotheistic
Nzambi
monogamous
polygamous
polytheistic
polyphonic
monophonic
hocket
simple melodic
  hocket
compound melodic
  hocket

tremolos
hemiola
molino
elima
lukembi
sanza
mbira
mapili
shaman
bull-roarer
azmari
Bushmen

Bibliography

BEBEY, FRANCIS, *African Music*. New York: Lawrence Hill & Co., 1975.

BRANDEL, ROSE, *The Music of Central Africa*. The Hague: Martinus Nijhoff, 1961.

———, "Types of Melodic Movement in Central Africa," *Ethnomusicology* 6(2—1962):75–87.

MERRIAM, ALAN P., *The Anthropology of Music*. Evanston, Illinois: Northwestern University Press, 1964

Discography

Ba-Benzele Pygmies. Recordings and commentary by Simkha Arom. UNESCO Collection. BM 30 L 2303.

The Music of the Dan. Recordings and notes by Hugo Zemp. UNESCO Collection. BM 30 L 2301.

The Music of Kung Bushmen of the Kalahari Desert, Africa. Recorded by John Phillipson. Edited by Moses Asch. Ethnic Folkways FE 4487.

Musique du Burundi. Recordings and commentary by Michel Vuylsteke. Descriptive notes in French and English. Ocora OCR 40.

Musique centrafricaine. Recordings and notes in French and English by Charles Duvelle. Ocora OCR 43.

II MUSICAL INSTRUMENTS

6 Idiophones

The study of musical instruments may be approached in the following four ways: (1) classification and construction, (2) social and artistic functions, (3) the music that instruments make, and (4) playing technique.

The study of the construction of musical instruments includes description of the materials used, measurements of the parts, and methods of construction. *Organology*, the scientific study of musical instruments, provides us with the facts concerning their classification, description, and measurements.[1] Musical instruments in general, on a worldwide basis, lend themselves to laboratory research. Visual information may easily be obtained by visiting museums or viewing the showcases of individual collectors, or it may be collected directly by the researcher in the field.

A system of classification that originated in India and was improved and later adopted by European musicologists is used almost universally to categorize musical instruments into four main classes: (1) *idiophones*, (2) *membranophones*, (3) *aerophones*, and (4) *chordophones*. A fifth class, *electrophones*, has been added for musical instruments that use electric power, such as electric guitars. This term can also be used to classify an instrument that produces sound electronically, such as the Moog and the electronic organ. As we prefer to use this classification for our present purposes, other existing systems will not be discussed here.[2]

[1]For a general knowledge, read Curt Sach's *History of Musical Instruments.*

[2]For other suggested systems of classification, see: Theodore C. Grame, "Bamboo and Music: A New Approach to Organology," pp. 142–149. Bruno Nettl, *Theory and Method in Ethnomusicology*, pp. 210–223.

Idiophones

Idiophones are instruments the vibrating bodies of which themselves produce sound. Marimbas, xylophones, gongs, metal and gourd rattles, bells, clappers, friction sticks, cymbals, and an endless variety of rubbed, scraped, and stamped instruments are all classified as idiophones. They are the most common of all African instruments. There are idiophones worn on the human body, attached to other objects including musical instruments, and shaken or struck by human hands. These idiophones that are shaken or struck by human hands, known as *primary idiophones*, are particularly important because they are extensively employed in the performance of African music and dance. They may be tuned or untuned. *Secondary idiophones* are often attached to other objects.

Tuned Idiophones

Tuned idiophones combine the rhythmic potentials of percussion and the melodic possibilities of tuned instruments. (Outside Africa, the Southeast Asian cultures, especially Indonesian and Cambodian, use a great variety of tuned idiophones in their ensembles.) Among the numerous tuned idiophones, we will introduce the three most important types: the hand-plucked *mbira*, the xylophone, and the stone chimes.

Technically included in the subclass *linguaphone*, the *mbira* is commonly described as a plucked idiophone. European travelers and missionaries have ethnocentrically called it "Kaffir piano" and "African piano." It has also been known by different African names such as *sanza, sansi, kalimba, likembe, lukembi, mbila,* and *kasansi*.[3] The problem of nomenclature is particularly difficult with this instrument because of the multitude of languages and dialects spoken by the peoples of sub-Saharan Africa. There is also as much diversity in the construction, type, and function of the *mbira* as there is in nomenclature.

Although widely distributed throughout Africa, the *mbira* is especially popular among the peoples living in and around Zambia, Zimbabwe, and Mozambique. The peoples of these regions are historically known for their metal craftsmanship. The *mbira* is the instrument par excellence of the Shona people of Zimbabwe who indeed favor the name *mbira*. Paul Berliner, a *mbira* player and author of an outstanding book on the subject titled *The Soul of Mbira*, said:

> The diaries of the first European missionaries and adventurers in southern Africa clearly indicate that the Shona were highly skilled blacksmiths and that the *mbira* was a well-established musical instrument among the Shona at least by the sixteenth century. More-

[3]Gerhard Kubik, "Generic Names for the Mbira," (1964) pp. 25–36 and (1965) pp. 72–73. See also Hugh Tracey, "A Case for the Name, Mbira," pp. 17–25.

over, it is most likely that the *mbira* was an important instrument among the Shona long before its first printed documentation. The Shona are believed to have settled in Zimbabwe as early as the tenth century, and the Early Iron Age itself dates back to the third century in Zimbabwe.[4]

The *mbira* generally consists of five parts: metal tongues or *lamellae*, a wooden soundboard, a bridge, a metal bar for restraining the tongues, and rattle or buzzing attachments. The lamellae or keys are often made of iron or brass; even umbrella wires and bicycle spokes are sometimes used. They vary in number, depending on the preferences of a particular ethnic group. The tuning of the *mbira* depends on the length, weight, and flexibility of these tongues. A pitch can be raised or lowered by filing, grinding, or slightly altering the vibrating length by hammering the tip or the bridge area of the lamellae. In some areas, such as Angola and Cameroon, wax may be stuck on the metal to lower the tone. The tips of the lamellae are always smooth to protect the safety of the performer's thumbs. These metal tongues are mounted on a wooden board, which is commonly rectangular or slightly flared in shape. In many *mbira*, the board is hollowed out to improve the resonance. The board is commonly placed inside a large hemispherical calabash, which acts as a resonator. A metal bar braces the lamellae over two bridges, which enable the lamellae to vibrate freely. The keys are arranged in a staggered order to give the performer's thumbs and fingers ample access. Rattles or jingles are mounted to add a

buzzing sound. The melodic sounds are produced when the player plucks the tuned metal keys with his thumbs and occasionally forefingers. The tuning of the *mbira* is determined chiefly by the length and width of the keys; it is also affected by the metal's mass and the presence or absence of wax.

The *mbira* is often played solo or to accompany the voice. In most cases, the performer is also a vocalist, and hence accompanies his singing on the *mbira*. A highly creative instrument, the *mbira* provides interesting chordal and melodic backgrounds that interact with the voice. The *mbira* is especially effective when it accompanies story-songs. Most *mbira*

Figure 6.1. Playing technique of mbira dzavadzimu. From Paul Berliner's The Soul of Mbira, © copyright 1978. Used by permission of the University of California Press.

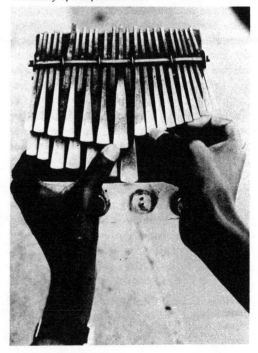

4Paul F. Berliner, *The Soul of Mbira*, p. 29.

players like to sing story-songs, epics, and ballads as well as to improvise songs of a personal nature while accompanying themselves. There is no limitation on the length of the performance, as long as the performer improvises and sings new ideas. Sometimes the listeners participate actively by repeating a refrain or a phrase in chorus.[5] Textual phrases accompanied by the *mbira* are commonly alternated with solo *mbira* passages. Laughing, singing, talking, whistling, and yodeling are traits of the vocalists.

The song texts are generally improvised and deal with a variety of subject that may be of a personal, social, or political nature. While much of the music performed on the *mbira* is secular, there are some *mbira* types associated primarily with spiritual or religious music. The Shona *mbira dzavadzimu*, for example, is often utilized in the performance of music involved with worship or appeasement of ancestral spirits; in fact, its name means "the *mbira* of the ancestral spirits."[6]

Paul Berliner demonstrates the tuning plan of *mbira dzavadzimu* as shown in the following diagram.[7] It must be stressed, however, that pitch relationships and intervals can sometimes differ greatly from one instrument to another. Consequently, the illustration serves a descriptive purpose only.

The African *xylophone* is an idiophone that consists of a series of tuned keys, usually wooden bars, which are arranged parallel to one another and mounted on a frame. (*Xylos* is Greek for "wood.") The number of bars varies from

culture to culture. Xylophones with only four bars are found among the Ibo of Nigeria and the Baule of the Ivory Coast. The xylophone with the widest compass—twenty-two bars—is occasionally found in East Africa among the Ganda of Uganda; it is called *akandinda*. The frames of xylophones are made of a variety of materials including tree trunks, banana stems, and large boxes. Even bundles of grass or a pit in the ground may be used. Another type of xylophone, for occasional performances, consists of tuned bars placed across human legs. Each type is known by its frame: *pit xylophone, box xylophone, leg xylophone, log xylophone*, and so on. Xylophones that have gourd resonators mounted on a frame and suspended under each tuned bar are known as *marimba*. Today the *marimba* is widely distributed throughout the world; it is actively used in the performance of African and African-derived music. European and American composers have often included it in contemporary works.

Wherever traditional xylophones are found—Nigeria, Ghana, Uganda, Zaire, Mozambique—they are most commonly played in small *ensembles* or groups of two, three, or four instruments. Although rare, large groups also exist. The best and the largest xylophone ensembles are found among the Chopi of Mozambique and may consist of as many as thirty performers. Xylophone ensembles often include other instruments— such as the *mbira*, drums, and other idiophones—to form an African version of an orchestra. These orchestras perform with dance groups. The Chopi of Mozambique are among the societies that are highly respected for their craftsmanship of, and performance on, a vari-

[5]Andrew Tracey, "The Mbira Music of Jege A. Tapera," pp. 44–63.

[6]Paul F. Berliner, *op. cit.*, p. 33.

[7]*Ibid.*, p. 55.

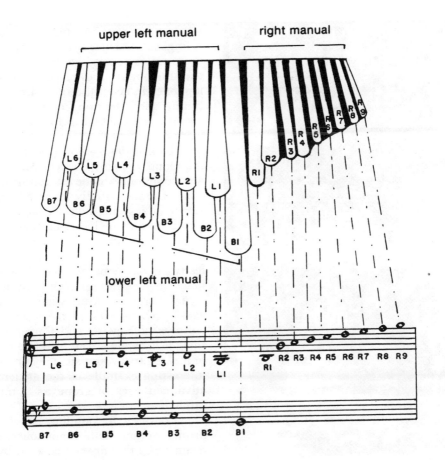

upper left manual

right manual

lower left manual

pitches in ascending order

Figure 6.2. Tuning system of mbira dzavadzimu.
From Paul Berliner's The Soul of Mbira, © *copyright 1978.*
Used by permission of the University of California Press.

tone) and *pentatonic* (five-tone) scales. It is important to note here that the tones of these scales do not exactly correspond to the European tempered scales. Xylophones in general require frequent retuning and attention because the tones become distorted when the bars become worn out, too dry, or moist.

Stone chimes, known as *lithophones*, are found in many parts of Africa. They are commonly made of basalt. Tuned stone chimes, usually four or five, with varying sizes and pitches, enable the performer to play melodies on them. Single stone chimes are used for signaling purposes. They call villagers to meetings, festivals, and emergencies. Among the black Jews of Ethiopia, they are used to signal a call to prayer. Stone chimes are also known to exist in the West African cultures of Nigeria and Cameroon. Although lithophones are rarely employed in making today's music, they provide an interesting example of the ancient and advanced uses of stone as a musical implement.

Contrary to popular belief, some drums are not membranophones. Those drum types that are not covered by skin or membrane are categorized as idiophones. The *clay-pot drums* found among the Ijaw and Ibo of Nigeria, for example, are idiophones. Pots of different sizes are filled with water to tune each drum to its appropriate pitch. The more water, the higher the pitch. These drums are played as an ensemble with special fans made from the frond of a palm or a coconut tree. Clay-pot idiophonic drums produce interesting tone qualities that can be easily differentiated from the conventional membranophones. (The slit-drum, which will be discussed later, is also an idiophone.)

*Figure 6.3. A xylophone and a variety of drums in the Sudan. *

ety of xylophones. Given the variety of musical instruments that are handmade (and not factory-produced), there are many ways of tuning xylophones. The tonal and artistic requirements of each instrument maker are decisive determinants of tuning. Each instrument maker in turn reflects the musical and tonal preferences of his society, of which he is an important part. Most xylophones, however, are tuned to *heptatonic* (seven-

54

Untuned Idiophones

For purposes of general identification and classification, untuned idiophones may be divided into instruments *with definite pitches* and those *with indefinite pitches*.

Untuned idiophones with definite pitches

The boat-shaped clapperless bell, popular in western Africa and known as *atoke* in Ghana,[8] is a good example of an untuned idiophone with a definite pitch. Its body, made entirely from iron, is struck on the side with a metal rod near the slit between the edges of the mouth. The instrument maker does not tune it, but because of its iron body it sounds a definite pitch.

There are many other types of clapperless bells, metal and wooden, with definite pitches, that are actively employed in the performance of African music. *Single* and *double* metal bells are among the most common. Two single bells of different sizes are soldered together to form a double bell. The player produces sounds by striking the body of the bell or bells with a metal or wooden beater. Of course, all these untuned idiophones are used solely as rhythm instruments.

Another popular instrument of North Africa is the *metal jingle*. A metal jingle is an idiophone with a container that holds a free single pellet. The container has a slit and a handle. It is believed that the bell is derived from the jingle. The ordinary bell has, of course, a

hanging clapper or tongue that is attached to the inside of its body.

The *slit-drum* is another untuned idiophone that falls into the category of instruments with definite pitches. It is made of a single, hollowed log of wood. As the name implies, a ˙section of the wood is slit open at the center, forming a pair of lips. Each lip sounds a definite pitch when it is struck with a beater. It is even possible to produce contrasting tones depending on the side of the instrument and the angle at which it is struck. Because of this ability to produce contrasting tones, the slit-drum has been used to transmit messages in African tone languages; the Lokele of Central Africa, for example, use them for such a purpose. Hence, it is sometimes referred to as a "talking drum" by many African societies. (It is important not to confuse this instrument with skin-covered drums.)

Untuned idiophones with indefinite pitches

Among the untuned idiophones, rattles are the most important. They are instruments of ancient origin. Three varieties of rattles are particularly important in African music: *net rattles*, *vessel rattles*, and *metal rattles*.

Hard objects such as seeds, nutshells, colorful beads, or animal teeth are woven together into a loose net that covers the outside of a gourd. The hollow gourd, which has been dried in the sun after the seeds were cleaned out, acts as a resonating body. The *shekere* or *sekere*, especially prevalent in Nigeria but now

[8]J.H.K. Nketia, *The Music of Africa*, pp. 69–81.

popular throughout the black world of Africa and America, represents the largest and the loudest of all African net rattles.

The net rattle may be played in many different ways. It can be tossed from one hand to another; it can be bounced up and down between a hand and a thigh; it can be shaken with both hands; or it can be tapped with the fingers of one or both hands. It plays intricate rhythms in the agile performance of a professional performer. The performer's coordination and skill are absolutely essential in producing the desired rattling sound in time to the rhythm of the music. This rattle is not played by women. In most cases, following the dictates of tradition, only professional musicians are permitted to own and play net rattles of the *shekere* type.

Container or vessel rattles, on the other hand, are chiefly used by women and children and not by male professional musicians. Vessel rattles are made of hollowed gourds. They are used as containers or vessels for hard objects. Women and children fill the empty gourds with pebbles, pellets, grain, or bones and shake them on important festive occasions and during national celebrations. Vessel rattles are popular throughout sub-Saharan Africa. Both net and vessel rattles are of great importance to the music and dance of numerous societies. Ingenious creativity is displayed in their construction as well as in their performance roles.

The Egyptian *temple sistrum* is probably the oldest and best-known idi-

Figure 6.5. Ethiopian sistrum (tsenatsil), silver, 18–19th century. Langmuir Collection no. 385. Photo by Mark Sexton. Reprinted by permission of the Peabody Museum of Salem.

ophone to Western musicologists. It is made of three or four metal rods that are horizontally drawn through a bow or U-shaped frame with a handle. However, the oldest Egyptian sistrum *(sakhm)* was made of wood, porcelain, or pottery. The more recent standard type *(saissit)* is made of metal. Both are equipped with movable discs, threaded on the rods, which jingle or clash when the instrument is shaken. It is interesting to note here that the ancient sistrums of Egyptian origin later spread to Greece, Rome, and other cultures around the Mediterranean as well as to other countries on the African continent.

Etymologically, the Egyptian word *saissit* stems from *seschesch*—a movement of young women in ancient Egyptian ritual who gathered water plants on the banks of the Nile to make rattling bouquets.[9] *(Sistrum* is a Latin term de-

rived from the Greek *seistron,* meaning "thing shaken.") It is used in Ethiopian Orthodox Christian churches as well as in the Fellasha synagogues, where it is known as *tsenatsil.* It is popular in many Jewish communities of North Africa and the Middle and Near East, where it accompanies sacred chants. An angle-shaped sistrum with calabash discs is found among a few tribes in West Africa. These societies include the Bambara of western Sudan; the Kissi, Malinke, and Boule of the Ivory Coast; and residents of the Bobo region of Nigeria. The instrument is used primarily in male circumcision and female excision rites. Sound is produced by means of concussion: the calabash discs rattle as they glide down the rod.

Secondary idiophones include not only instruments that are played independently but also those that are worn on the human body or attached to other objects. In order to accentuate their body

[9]Bertil Soderberg, "The Sistrum," pp. 91–133.

Figure 6.6. Ethiopian priests of the Christian Church chanting, accompanied by sistrum, drum, and sticks. Research on the Fellasha funded by NEA. Photo by A. Kebede. All rights reserved, Ashenafi Kebede Collection.

movements as well as provide rhythmic accompaniment to the music, dancers all over Africa wear idiophones, such as *ankle rattles, leg rattles, waist rattles,* and *wrist rattles. Ankle rattles* consist of brass bells attached to leather strips that are tied around the ankle. There are also other varieties commonly worn by girls and boys when they go to weddings or other occasions where dancing is an important part of the festivity. Only in rare instances are ankle rattles worn by men; the Watutsi spear dancer is one such case.

The most common *leg rattle* is made of empty cocoon shells filled with pebbles and strung on two cords of fiber. It is wound around the legs of each performer and securely tied in position. Although the cocoons are gathered by girls and the leg rattles made by women, they are worn mostly by men for specialized male hunting dances. The women cut a hole in each cocoon, and a small stone or pebble is placed inside it. A pair of cocoons is sewn to a long cord of plaited fiber or strung on strips of leather. As many as one hundred fifty cocoons are used, and each leg rattle is about two yards long.[10]

Waist rattles are made of the hooves of animals (antelopes or goats, for example), bells, or jingles. They are suspended from a leather or thin fiber belt. Their most important function is to accentuate the dancer's hip movements. Among the Xhosa of South Africa, there are rattles that consist of a number of dry gourds fastened around the waist of the dancer. Waist rattles are commonly worn by women, especially those of marriageable age.

Wrist rattles are frequently worn by African doctors and healers. They are made like ankle rattles and their variants. Some wrist rattles are made of little leather bags, each of which contains a few stones. The bags are secured to bands of leather and fastened to the wrist (or ankle) of the dancer. When the leather bags dry they become stiff and sound slightly sonorous when shaken. It is important to point out that most of these secondary idiophones, worn on the dancers' bodies, have functions both decorative and musical. Dancers also wear rattling necklaces made of bamboo, animal hooves, and other decorative materials. The idiophones worn on the human body discussed so far are found among many societies of sub-Saharan Africa; Bushmen, Watutsi, Baganda, and Xhosa peoples have a large variety of rattles.

Castanets, idiophonic finger rings usually worn on the thumb and middle fingers, had a role in ancient Egyptian musical practices. They were used by dancing girls to entertain the pharaohs for hundreds of years before and during the Christian era. Castanets consist of two discs connected by a cord; there are many varieties and sizes. The wooden type has a powerful resonance when clicked together (this is the type popular in modern Spanish music). Iron castanets are found today in West African dance music; these idiophones sound like bells. And, like most idiophones worn by humans, they are chiefly dancers' instruments. They enhance the vitality of the rhythm in coordination with body movement.

Musical instruments with idiophone attachments include *tambourines*, which have circular jingles, and the harps of Zaire, which are also provided with jingles.

The *scraper*, a piece of wood or bone with a corrugated surface, produces a rasping sound when it is rubbed by a stick. This simple instrument is popularly used in most dance ensembles of sub-Saharan Africa; African-derived peoples of North and South America actively use the scraper in their dance bands, as is the case in Haiti, Cuba, and Trinidad. (The modern type, known as *güiro*, has even made its way into the European symphony orchestra.)

Africans generally make idiophonic instruments directly from material they find around them. A *pair of sticks* is hit together to mark the dance rhythms of most ensembles. Single or double sticks are used to beat on other objects including drums, bells, or logs. Empty shoe-polish tins, cans, and bottles may be filled with stones, animal teeth, sand, grain, and other objects to form rattles. Animal horns and bones are turned into scrapers. The ground is beaten with long poles, for example, during funeral ceremonials as part of the death dance. The list of improvised instruments is endless!

---

[10]Information about and beautiful pictures of rattles are found in Francis Bebey's *African Music*.

Basic Terms

If you aren't sure what each of the following terms means, look back at the text, where they appear in italic type. Additional information about some of them may also be found by checking the index.

organology	stone chimes
electrophones	lithophones
idiophones	clay-pot drums
primary idiophones	atoke
secondary idiophones	single metal bells
tuned idiophones	double metal bells
linguaphone	metal jingle
mbira	slit-drum
sanza	shekere
sansi	sekere
kalimba	net rattle
likembe	vessel rattle
lukembi	temple sistrum
mbila	sakhm
kasansi	saissit
lamellae	tsenatsil
mbira dzavadzimu	ankle rattle
xylophone	leg rattle
akandinda	waist rattle
marimba	wrist rattle
ensembles	castanets
heptatonic	scraper
pentatonic	güiro

Bibliography

BEBEY, FRANCIS, *African Music*. New York: Lawrence Hill & Co., 1975.

BERLINER, PAUL F., *The Soul of Mbira*. Los Angeles: University of California Press, 1978.

———,*CHOPI MUSICIANS*. LONDON: OXFORD UNIVERSITY PRESS, 1970.

GRAME, THEODORE C., "Bamboo and Music: A New Approach to Organology," *Readings in Ethnomusicology*, ed. David P. McAllester. New York: Johnson Reprint Corporation, 1971, pp. 142–149.

KUBIK, GERHARD, "Generic Names for the Mbira," *African Music Society Journal* 3 (3—1964):25–36.

———, "Generic Names for the Mbira," *African Music Society Journal* 3 (4—1965):72–73.

NETTL, BRUNO, *Theory and Method in Ethnomusicology*. London: The Free Press of Glencoe, 1964.

NKETIA, J.H. KWABENA, *The Music of Africa*. New York: W.W. Norton & Co., 1974.

SACHS, CURT, *The History of Musical Instruments*. New York: W.W. Norton & Co., 1940.

SODERBERG, BERTIL, "The Sistrum: A Musicological Study," *Ethnos* (Stockholm) 33 (1–4, 1969):90–133.

TRACEY, ANDREW, "The Matepe Mbira Music of Rhodesia," *African Music Society Journal* 4 (4—1970):37–61.

———, "The Mbira Music of Jege A. Tapera," *African Music Society Journal* 2 (4—1961):24–28.

TRACEY, HUGH, "A Case for the Name, Mbira," *African Music Society Journal* 2(4—1961):17–25.

———, *Chopi Musicians*. London: Oxford University Press, 1970.

Discography

Mbira Music of Rhodesia. Introduction by Robert Kauffman. Performed by Abraham Dumisani Maraire. Ethnic Music Series. University of Washington Press, Seattle, Washington. UPW-1001.

The Music of Africa Series. Musical Instruments 5. Xylophones. Recordings and commentary by Hugh Tracey. Kalidophone Records KMA 5.

Musique centrafricaine. Recording and commentary by Charles Duvelle. Ocora OCR 43. (Side one, band 1 provides a rare combination of xylophone and *mbira* and band 6 an example of a pit xylophone and xylophone with resonators.)

Shona Mbira Music. Field-recorded by Paul Berliner. Nonesuch Explorer Series. Nonesuch H-72077.

The Soul of Mbira: Traditions of the Shona People of Rhodesia. Field recorded by Paul Berliner. Nonesuch Explorer Series. Nonesuch H-72054.

7 Membranophones

In African music, especially in the styles of music performed south of the Sahara, membranophones are second in importance to idiophones. *Membranophones* are drums with skin or membrane heads. (Drums without membranes, such as clay-pot drums, are categorized as idiophones.) There are many different kinds of drums. The same kind of drum, with small variations in construction and with a different name, can often be found used by many ethnic groups. In other words, each tribe or language group has a name for every instrument. And yet, some areas have more drums than others. East Africa, for example, has more types of drums than West Africa. This survey provides an overview of the existing variety of drums and cites the better-known types as examples.

Let us consider identifying drums according to their size, shape, and material. There are drums that stand ten to

fifteen feet tall, carved from the trunks of trees; the performers play them standing on platforms built behind the drums. At the other extreme, there are drums made of coconut shells small enough to hold in one hand.

As to materials, membranophones can be made of hollow tree trunks or of staves of wood bound together with iron hoops. Many kinds of wood are used. Other drums are made of metal, bone, gourd, nutshell, and clay. In Ghana and Kenya, tins are used today instead of the traditional hard-fruit shells. Oxhide, calf, goat, elephant, or lizard skin may be used to cover the frame, depending on the geographic location and availability of the animal.

Membranophones are loosely divided into three main categories: *tubular drums, bowl-shaped drums,* and *friction drums.*

Tubular drums are made in many

Figure 7.1. Sudanese instruments. The slit-drum can be clearly seen at the center of the membranophones. Mission to the Sudan funded by UNESCO. Photo by A. Kebede. All rights reserved. Ashenafi Kebede Collection.

with leather cord on top of the wooden body. Suspended horizontally from a strap around the player's shoulders, the drum is struck by both bare hands on its two heads or faces, the right hand playing on the larger face and the left hand on the smaller. The small face produces a higher tone than the large one.

Other membranophones in the oriental African zone include the *naqqara* and the *tar.* The term *naqqara* designates double kettledrums used in North African kingdoms, as among the Tauregs of the Sahara. These drums symbolize the power of the king and are often left standing near the throne. They were sometimes used to accompany imperial proclamations before the advent of technological communication. The *negarit* serves similar purposes in Ethiopia; in fact, the name is derived from the Amharic verb *negere* which means "talked" or "proclaimed." Etymologically, *naqqara* is a cognate of the Ethiopian *negarit* and the English *nakers.* The *tar* is a tambourine popular in the music cultures of North Africa, the Middle and Near East. It plays an important part in the rhythmic sections of Andalusian classical music of Tunisia and Morocco. The Halfaya people of the Sudan use *tar* to accompany their secular songs and dances. Tambourines, fitted with idiophonic attachments around their edges, such as circular jingles are commonly used in Egypt to accompany belly dancers.

The most beautiful types of *double-headed drums* are popularly found in Uganda and the Great Lake regions. Each drum has two heads, although sometimes the bottom skin is not playable. The top face is larger than the bottom face. These double-headed drums

forms, including those that resemble the shapes of a barrel, cylinder, goblet, cone, and hourglass. The Ethiopian *kebero*, a religious processional drum type also found in Egypt and Sudan, is an excellent example of a large double-headed cylindrical drum. It is made of a hollowed-out log. The interior and exterior are iron-filed and smoothed with sandpaper. The two open faces, one smaller than the other, are covered with pieces of oxhide. The skins are first treated with animal fat to prevent them from cracking. Then they are stretched and laced are structurally laced. The skins of both faces are joined together by ropes laced around the drum from top to bottom. Hence, almost the entire wooden body is beautifully covered by skins.

Almost all African societies possess drums. With a few exceptions, the drum is the most popular instrument south of the Sahara. (In northwestern Ghana, for example, the xylophone has more musical significance than the drum.) In recent years, knowledge about the musical instruments of sub-Saharan cultures has been widely disseminated by native African writers and musicologists. A great deal is known about the *atumpan* through the articles of Kwabena Nketia, a prominent Ghanaian musicologist and author of the book *The Music of Africa*. A film about the *atumpan* has been made by the eminent American ethnomusicologist Mantle Hood. The single-headed *atumpan* is the master drum of the Ashanti tribe; today it is also played in all Akan communities of West Africa. It is made of a single hollowed-out piece of durable wood of the *tweneboa* tree. The single skin is held by ropes or metal strings laced onto wooden pegs; the pegs are anchored in the body of the *atumpan*. Because of its association with high office, the making of the *atumpan* drum is initiated following an intricate ceremony. A tree has to be chosen in an appropriate location (not one located on or near crossroads). Before it is cut down, libations have to be poured to placate the spirit inhabiting the tree. Then the body of the drum will be prepared by a specialized woodcarver. Following the dictates of tradition, the woodcarver will draw an "eye" on the frame of the drum that always stares in the direction of the drummer. This watchful "eye" is in-

tended to prevent misuse and foul play on the drum as well as to enable the master drummer to commune with the patron deity of music.[1]

The installation of a new paramount chief cannot take place without a pair of new *atumpan* drums and their active participation in the ceremonial music. The master drum is used to play in three contexts: the dance mode, the signal mode, and the speech mode.[2] This drum accompanies dances when it is played in the first mode. It also plays in the signal mode when leading other instruments in ensemble performance. There is a difference between drum signaling and drum "talking." In drum signaling, the aim is to announce something or give a warning. This is in principle similar to the drum signals used in European military operations and to bugle calls. In drum talking, however, the human language is imitated and codified. Contrary to some claims, one is not limited to a few phrases. Almost any situation or topic can be conveyed on a drum by a good drummer to listeners who understand the language. The underlying principle by which drum messages can be sent depends on the nature of African tonal languages. Following the high-low pitches of the tone language, the *atumpan* recites proverbs, poems, and praises of the chief, the valor of warriors, or the memory of ancestor drummers. Contemporary uses have been found for the *atumpan:* every year in Accra, the capital of Ghana, the *atum-*

[1]*Africa East and West.* Recording edited and narrated by Mantle Hood. See also *Atumpan,* film produced by Mantle Hood.

[2]*Ibid.* The film *Atumpan* is recommended for class viewing during a lesson on West African drums, drummaking, and performance.

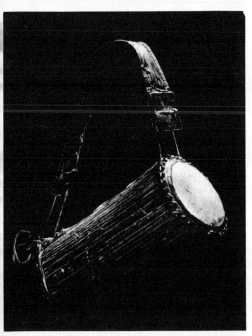

Figure 7.2. Hourglass or pressure drum. Photo by Harry Knight, Exton Studio. Armer Collection of Nigerian Artifacts. © Copyright 1980 FSU Center for Black Culture. Used by permission of the FSU Center for Black Culture.

pan is used to open parliament. The drums are also heard on the radio to announce news broadcasts. Talking drums are used in pairs, one for the high note and another for the low. The Ashanti and Ewe people of Ghana are notable users of talking drums. In general, talking drums are more common in West and Central Africa than in the rest of the continent.

The drum languages are played on a variety of drums, including the *hourglass drum*. Its name is derived from the shape of its body, which resembles the European hourglass. Though double-headed, only one face of the drum is played. Variations in pitch are obtained by tight-ening or loosening the drum head. The more tension, the higher the resultant tone. For instant tuning, the hourglass drum is placed under the armpit of the performer; this position of the drum will enable him to apply different degrees of pressure on the lacings. Consequently, it is also known as a *pressure drum*. It is a drum type that is widely distributed in both oriental and sub-Saharan cultures of Africa. Today it is even gaining popularity among the African-derived peoples in the Western Hemisphere, such as black Americans, West Indians, and Afro-Cubans.

The preceding discussion of talking drums and tone languages is directly related to *pitch*, the highness or lowness of a tone. The *timbre*, or tone quality, and pitch of a drum are influenced by many factors: size and shape, the materials used in construction, and the way the drum is held and played. Even the shape of the sticks used to beat the drum is carefully chosen with the desired sonority in mind. The sticks may be straight or curved, with or without knobs at the ends. The weight, length, thickness, and hardness of the sticks are important, too. Different sticks are made from different kinds of wood. A particular drum must be played with the correct sticks; otherwise the wrong tone will result. Differences in tone quality and pitch are also obtained by playing the drum with the bare hand, held in various positions, or by a combination of hand and stick.

Tone is also affected by the way in which the drum head is fixed. The skin may be glued, nailed, lapped, or laced. In other drums, such as the *atumpan*, the skin is suspended on pegs that can be pushed in or out to regulate the tension.

Sometimes the head is laced to a ring at the bottom of the drum, or, in double-headed drums such as the hourglass drum, to another skin.

The body of the friction drum type, the last category, is made either of clay or wood. It is covered by a thin membrane with a small perforation in the center. A straw or cord passes through this hole and attaches to the underside, holding the membrane taut. Sound is produced by rubbing the drum head with a stick, damp fingers, or sometimes both. Of course, variations of pitch are dependent upon the speed and pressure of the performer's fingers moving along the straw. The friction drum is commonly found in most sub-Saharan cultures and has diverse symbolic attributes and tonal representations. The *etwie* of Ghana imitates a leopard's snarl.[3]

Drum Ensembles

The drum is commonly played in ensembles. To achieve tonal contrast in a drum ensemble, it is necessary to combine at least three drums: high-, medium-, and low-pitched. Some drum ensembles may have more than twenty drums that are beaten together for some special event. Examples of large drum ensembles include the bands of hourglass drums of the *Dagomba* in Ghana and the Yoruba in Nigeria, the ensemble of fifteen *entenga* drums of Uganda, the clay-pot drums of the Ijaw and Ibo in Nigeria, and the Akan (Ghana) ensemble of hourglass, gourd, and double-headed cylindrical drums.

Sometimes a drum orchestra is combined with a chorus of male or female singers, or both. This occurs in certain traditional associations, cults, and warrior and hunter organizations. Drums are also played in combination with other instruments. Groups of drums, from two to nine, are played together with a variety of idiophones, such as gongs and rattles. Ensembles of drums and xylophones are popular throughout sub-Saharan Africa. Any combination of aerophones, chordophones, and idiophones may be played with drums.

Among the most important orchestras in Africa are those of the Chopi in southeastern Africa and of the Baganda in Central Africa. In addition to drums, these orchestras include singers, a xylophone section, and rattles. The Chopi orchestra has two drums, a big and a small one. The Baganda orchestra uses four drums. Usually the first drum keeps a steady beat while the second syncopates; the third and fourth drums play highly improvised rhythmic passages.

The leader of a drum ensemble is a well-qualified performer. He is versed in the oral literature and history of his society. He is required to sing in a pleasant voice. His wrist must be flexible, and he must be skilled in the dynamics of the drum and the techniques of tone production.

[3]J.H.K. Nketia, *The Music of Africa*, p. 91.

Tuned drums play melodic passages. The fifteen-drum *entenga* ensemble of Uganda plays tunes similar in structure and form to those played on xylophones. The drums are tuned to definite pitches. Three of the drums constitute the rhythm section and are played by two drummers: one drummer plays only one drum, while the second drummer plays the other two drums of varying sizes. The remaining twelve drums have the melody. Four drummers are used for this section, each one playing a set of three drums.

Drums in Religious Ceremony

Drums play an important role in African religious ceremonies. The Sudanese Dervish sect performs its ritual songs and dances accompanied by drums; intricate dance movements and syncopated rhythms are performed simultaneously each Friday afternoon at the Hamad el Nil cemetery in Omdurman. In Egypt, drums play an important role during the religious ceremonies of the Sufi mystic brotherhood in Cairo. Priests of the Ethiopian and Coptic Christian Churches undertake specialized training in order to master the techniques employed in playing the drums that accompany sacred hymns sung during the year.

Basic Terms

If you aren't sure what each of the following terms means, look back at the text, where they appear in italic type. Additional information about some of them may also be found by checking the index.

membranophones	hourglass drum
kebero	pressure drum
naqqara	pitch
tar	timbre
negarit	etwie
double-headed drum	entenga
atumpan	

Bibliography

Atumpan: The Story and Sounds of the Talking Master Drum of the Ashanti. Film produced by Mantle Hood. 42 minutes, color, sound. Institute of Ethnomusicology, UCLA.

NKETIA, J.H. KWABENA, *The Music of Africa.* New York: W.W. Norton & Co., 1974.

Discography

Africa East and West. Edited by Mantle Hood, with narration by Hood and others. Institute of Ethnomusicology, UCLA. IER 6751.

Drums of the Yoruba of Nigeria. Ethnic Folkways Library FE 4441.

Folk Music of Western Congo. Recordings by Leo A. Verwilghen. Ethnic Folkways Library FE 4427.

The Music of Africa Series: Drums. Hugh Tracey. The International Library of African Music. Roodepoort, No. 29. GALP 1324.

The Music of the Dan. Recordings and commentary by Hugo Zemp. UNESCO Collection. BM 30 L 2301. (Play band 3 for a very good example of polyrhythmic drumming between three drummers.)

8 Aerophones

The instruments in the *aerophone* class produce sound when a column of air vibrates within a pipe. There are three types of aerophones: flutes and whistles, single- and double-reed pipes, and horns and trumpets.

Flutes and Whistles

The most widely distributed flutes around the world are made of bamboo; they are popularly found wherever bamboo grows. Bamboo is, of course, a grass, and like most members of its family, it is extremely hardy and of exceedingly wide distribution. It grows wild around the banks of rivers, lakes, springs, and their tributaries.[1]

The simplest flutes use bamboo tubes without finger holes. Each flute plays one pitch; hence, several performers with instruments of different pitches are required to play a melody. This technique of playing melodies by alternating instruments is known as *hocket;* it is a technique found in the performance of both instrumental and vocal music. The Ethiopian *embilta,* which is made of either bamboo or metal, is a good example of a flute without finger holes.

The panpipes, on the other hand, consisting of several single-pitch tubes

[1] See Theodore C. Grame, "Bamboo and Music," p. 142.

69

bound together usually in the form of a raft, are played by one or a group of performers. They are found among the Soga of Uganda, the Yombe of Zaire, and the Pedi of South Africa.

The oldest flutes with finger holes have been found in Egypt along the banks of the Nile. Early Egyptian paintings show the flute more than any other instrument.

> In one of the tombs in the Gizeh Pyramid (c. 2000 B.C.) a band of seven players is depicted performing on slanting flutes of various lengths, accompanying a soloist who is standing, the rest being either on their knees or sitting.[2]

Variations in the length of flutes are made by the performers who often make their own instruments. Hence differences in range, timbre, and relative pitch between flutes are attributed to differences in the quality of the bamboo used, differences in construction, variations in the length and width of the bamboo, and differences in the method of tone production (embouchure) and fingering techniques of the performer. Variations also exist in the distances between the finger holes. Sometimes the size of the hole itself depends on the size of the performer's fingers. Consequently, it is hardly possible to find in Africa two flutes that can play in perfect unison with uniform fingering. This also explains why the flute is more popular in the solo traditions of northern and northeastern Africa than in sub-Saharan Africa.

The Egyptian *sib* is an end-blown flute; that is, air is blown obliquely across the rim of one open end in order to

[2]H. Macaulay Fitzgibbon, *The Story of the Flute*, p. 4.

70

Figure 8.1. Washint player. Photo by A. Kebede. All rights reserved, Ashenafi Kebede Collection.

produce sounds. It is usually held at an angular position to the right of the player. Tonal expression and subtle ornamentation could be well executed by varying the angle of blowing against the open edge. Describing the Egyptian flute, Curt Sachs writes that "no instrument had a more incorporeal sound, a sweeter *sostenuto*, a more heart-felt *vibrato*."[3] *Nay* is a name that applies to a similar instrument in Tunisia and many other countries of the Muslim world, including Sudan and Algeria.[4] The five or six finger holes enable the performer to improvise melodies and to accompany vocal music in a characteristically elaborate style. In Morocco, a long flute *(awad)*, with a low

[3]See Curt Sach's *History of Musical Instruments*, p. 90.

[4]Play side one, band 1 of the UNESCO recording *Tunisia* for an excellent *nay* solo by Mr. Salah el Mahdi. Note also that in this scale or mode the third and seventh degree are neutral in ascending and that the seventh becomes a minor seventh in descending.

droning sound, is played by camel drivers to mitigate the solitude of the desert nights.

In Ethiopia, bamboo is found particularly concentrated around the regions of Lake Tana and the Atbara, Wabi Shebelai, Awash, and Abbay (Nile) rivers. As these fertile regions are also used for grazing cattle, it is no wonder that the flute has been closely associated with fertility and is commonly identified as a shepherd's instrument. In the Amhara music of Ethiopia, more than one *washint* flute with finger holes is not often encountered. Michael Powne seems to have observed this in his study when he writes the following:

A player who had made a number of his own instruments *(washints)* previously from segmented cane should readily be able to position the holes by eye, without the guiding rings. Slight variation or inaccuracy would not matter, as it is very infrequently that washints are played in consort.[5]

The average length of the *washint* is between sixteen and eighteen inches; traditionally, the length is measured by the number of rings or nodes on the bamboo.[6]

[5]Michael Powne, *Ethiopian Music*, p. 29.
[6]Play side one, band 1 of *Ethiopia: Azmari Music of the Amharas* for a sound example of the *washint*, played by Melaku Gelaw.

Figure 8.2. Aerophone players. From a traditional Ethiopian color painting. All rights reserved, Ashenafi Kebede Collection.

Among the Bashi of eastern Zaire, the *mulizi*, a notched, end-blown flute with finger holes, is popularly played by cattle herders. In addition to the flute melody, the performer is here required to hum simultaneously. According to Merriam:

> ...good and poor mulizi players are differentiated on the basis of their ability to produce a larynx tone coterminously with the flute tone. This tone, while akin to humming, is considerably more forceful and much rougher than the normal humming sound. Not all musicians are capable of producing it, and those who cannot are relegated to secondary status.[7]

The physical requirements involved in playing the *mulizi* are difficult to achieve; while the lips must be kept relatively relaxed in order to produce the flute melody, the larynx and diaphragm must be tense in order to produce the rough and throaty hum.

The easiest aerophone to play is a whistle, which consists of a single stopped pipe. It is blown at the open end. Whistles can be made of bamboo, wood, or metal. Empty glass bottles also make good whistles. The Swazi, for example, have whistles *(luveve)* made of either a small antelope horn or wood. It is primarily used for signaling purposes, to indicate the beginning of a hunt or to alert dogs to catch the quarry. Although whistles are found all over the world, their function in the creation of music is very limited.

Single- and Double-Reed Aerophones

Again, Egyptian studies provide us with a rich source of information in regard to ancient musical instruments recovered through archaeology. Because of the aridity of Egyptian soil, hundreds of instruments have been saved from decomposition. Undoubtedly the Egyptians' belief in reincarnation or afterlife and careful treatment of personal belongings before burial have greatly contributed to the preservation of musical instruments and other artistic works. For example, single- and double-reed pipes are shown in reliefs from the Old Kingdom.

In an example found as early as ca. 2700 B.C., a piper is depicted with a

[7]Alan P. Merriam, "The Bashi Mulizi and Its Music," p. 144.

double-pipe instrument *(memet)*; his fingers are positioned on the right-hand pipe. Obviously, the pipe on the left was used to play a drone to accompany the melody played on the other pipe. This *double clarinet*, sometimes mislabeled double flute or double reed (oboe), is today a common pan-Islamic aerophone. The reader should note here that a clarinet is identified by its *single* free reed. With its five or six fingerholes, it plays melodies with a range of six or seven notes. *Argul* is its most common name, but it is also known as *yarul*, *samr* (or *zamur)*, and *mashura*.

The reed pipe of the clarinet type produces sound when the performer blows air into a mouthpiece that has a single reed. It is not commonly used in the music of most societies of sub-Saharan Africa. However, it occurs in some parts of West Africa, particularly in Upper Volta, northern Ghana, Benin, and Chad.

The most common and popular *double reed* in North African music is the *zorna*. With its seven holes on top and an octave hole at the back, it plays highly ornamented melodies with a wide range.[8] The performer often uses his cheeks as an air reservoir or air bag to play *legato* passages or sustained tones with an incredibly long duration. Well known for their advanced breathing techniques, the performers are able to inhale air through their noses while simultaneously exhaling through their instruments.[9] This technique is known as "nosel" or "circular" breathing. Because of its loud volume and nasal tone, the *zorna* accompanies most festive occasions, such as weddings and births. A typical instrument of pan-Islamic music, it is also known by the names *gaita*, *al-keita*, and similar terms. Etymologically, its Tunisian name, *zorna*, is a variant of the Turkish name *zurna* and the Iranian *surnay*.

The double-reed aerophone appears in many societies of sub-Saharan Africa where the Islamic tradition has flourished. In the central African republic of Chad, it plays a leading role in ensemble performances. The same oboe type is found in Sudan, where it is closely associated with a dance called the *zihee* (circle dance). Other areas of Islamic penetration where the instrument appears include Somalia, Kenya, Tanzania, and Cameroon. It is also very popular among the Hausa of norther Nigeria.

Figure 8.3. West African double-reed argul players. Armer Collection of Nigerian Artifacts. All rights reserved, FSU Center for Black Culture.

Trumpets and Horns

African trumpets and horns use pipes or tubes made of bamboo, gourd, elephant tusks, animal horns, wood, or metal. The Mangbetus of central Africa use an ivory trumpet. Wooden trumpets are found in northern Ghana and in Zaire.

Of all aerophones, the manner of producing sound is probably most diffi-

---

[8]*Tunisia*, the UNESCO recording, contains an example of music played on *zorna* (or *zoukra*).

[9]Play side one, band 6 of the recording *The Master Musicians of Jajouka*. In this sound example three

al-keitas or *rhaitas* are played. Listen to the player who maintains the continuous drone by means of circular breathing toward the end of the piece.

Figure 8.4. Waza trumpets of the Sudanese Berta people, Mission to the Sudan funded by UNESCO. Photo by A. Kebede. All rights reserved, Ashenafi Kebede Collection.

cult on trumpets and horns. The tightly stretched lips of the performer induce the air in the column to vibrate and produce sound. Sound is produced by buzzing the lips. Changes in pitch are produced by varying the tension of the lips and force of breath as well as by varying the length of the vibrating air column in the tube by means of finger holes (or other mechanical devices as on modern European brass instruments). Most African trumpets have no finger holes. They are either end-blown or side-blown.

The Berta tribe of eastern Sudan has interesting *end-blown trumpets (waza)* made of gourd tubes stuck together with beeswax and tied with strings and thin slices of bamboo. The mouthpieces are also made of gourd. Since each instrument produces a single tone, ten *waza*, each with its own individual pitch, often perform as a group in the hocket style. The longest instrument,

Figure 8.5. Adolo horn of the Sudan. Photo by Amin Ahmed El Sayed. All rights reserved, Ashenafi Kebede Collection, FSU Center for Black Culture.

which plays the lowest tone, is about seven feet long, with a bottom diameter of eight inches, and a mouthpiece diameter of about two inches. A similar style is popular in neighboring Ethiopia, where the trumpets *(meleket* or *malakat)* are made either of bamboo or metal; they are often covered with leather. Other similar trumpets are found and widely used in Uganda, Tanzania, Chad, and especially among the Hausa of Nigeria, who favor a straight metal trumpet *(kakaki)* up to nine feet long.[10]

Trumpets made of animal horns and elephant tusks are generally intended to be side-blown. All the Bantu peoples use animal horns, especially those of antelopes *(phalaphala)*, as signal trumpets. However, individual ownership of these instruments is not permitted; they all belong to the community or village. These trumpets are usually played only by men on special occasions and for official purposes: to sound an alarm or to call warriors to arms. Hence, their usefulness as instruments of music is rather limited.

Basic Terms

If you aren't sure what each of the following terms means, look back at the text, where they appear in italic type. Additional information about some of them may also be found by checking the index.

aerophone	zamur
hocket	mashura
embilta	zorna
sib	legato
nay	gaita
awad	al-keita
washint	zihee

mulizi	end-blown trumpets
luveve	waza
memet	meleket
double clarinet	malakat
argul	kakaki
yarul	phalaphala
samr	

[10]For sound examples of trumpets and horns, play side two, band 2 of *An Anthology of African Music: Nigeria—Hausa Music I* and side two, band 2 of *Ethiopie: Polyphonies et techniques vocales;* play also side one, band 4 of *Musique centrafricaine,* which has an excellent example of an ensemble of four small horns and eight large wooden trumpets of different sizes; the build-up of harmonic sound is remarkably demonstrated.

Bibliography

FITZGIBBON, H. MACAULAY, *The Story of the Flute.* London: William Reeves Bookseller Limited, 1929.

GRAME, THEODORE C., "Bamboo and Music: A New Approach to Organology," *Readings in Ethnomusicology,* ed. David P. McAllester. New York: Johnson Reprint Corp., 1971, pp. 142–149.

MERRIAM, ALAN P., "The Bashi Mulizi and Its Music: An End-blown Flute from the Belgian Congo," *Journal of American Folklore* 70(1957):(143–56).

POWNE, MICHAEL, *Ethiopian Music: An Intro-*

duction. London: Oxford University Press, 1968.

SACHS, CURT, *The History of Musical Instruments*. New York: W.W. Norton & Co., 1940.

Discography

An Anthology of African Music: Nigeria—Hausa Music I. UNESCO Collection. BM 30 L 2306.

Ethiopie: Polyphonies et techniques vocales. Recording and notes by Jean Jenkins. Ocora OCR 44.

The Master Musicians of Jajouka: The Primal Energy That Is the Music and Ritual of Jajouka, Morocco. Produced by Joel Rubiner. Adelphi Records.

The Music of Africa Series. Flutes and Horns. Hugh Tracey. The International Library of African Music. Roodepoort, No. 30. GALP 1325.

The Music of Ethiopia: Azmari Music of the Amharas. Recordings and notes by Ashenafi Kebede. Anthology Records AST-6000.

Musique centrafricaine. Recording and commentary by Charles Duvelle, Ocora OCR 43.

Tunisia. Recordings and notes by Alain Daniélou. UNESCO Collection. BM 30 L 2008.

9 Chordophones

Stringed instruments or *chordophones* generally play more important roles in the music traditions of oriental Africa than in the traditions of sub-Saharan Africa. The social preference and performance practice of the northern cultures place emphasis on melodic more than on rhythmic elaboration. Consequently, we find a wealth of chordophones and aerophones in the oriental African zone.

The main four subclasses of stringed instruments are *lutes*, *lyres*, *zithers*, and *harps*. There are also instruments that combine the structural characteristics of two subclasses, as in harp-lutes and lyre-zithers.

Lutes

Lutes are divided into *plucked* and *bowed* types. A *fiddle* is a bowed lute.

Early Egyptian paintings in the Musée du Caire in Cairo depict *plucked lutes* played by women. Although the active role of women in musical entertainment has gradually disappeared along with imperial patronage, it is obvious that lute-type instruments, which resemble the modern banjo or guitar and were played with plectrum or quill, existed in pre-Christian times.

The short-necked *'ud* (from which the word *lute* derives) is today the foremost instrument of Islamic music in general. The Tunisian *'ud* has from four to

77

Figure 9.1. The 'ud. The Metropolitan Museum of Art, Gift of Dr. George C. Valliant, Miss Marian Valliant, and Mrs. Benjamin Tenney, Jr., in memory of Mr. Louis D. Valliant, 1944. All rights reserved, the Metropolitan Museum of Art.

societies such as those found in Ethiopia, it is an instrument widely used in the musical performances of most eastern African cultures.[1]

The body of the fiddle is made of a rectangular-, bowl-, or diamond-shaped frame. This frame is then covered with parchment or hide. Two corners of the frame are left with measured openings, opposite each other, in which the wooden neck is inserted. Two pieces of parchment of equal size are tightly stitched around the sides of the frame to form a hollowed and open inside. Then one to four sound holes are cut at the corners.

The neck is either a rounded or a rectangular piece of wood that is often decorated with carved or burned-in designs. This neck is generally made of one piece of wood; it is characteristically longer than the body. Quite often, the strings are made from strands of horsetail.

The curved horsehair bow is always treated with rosin before playing. It is held in a horizontal position. To produce special sound effects, slides, microtonal inflections, and decorative nuances, the angle of playing and the position of the hand are important factors. Bow pressure on the string also affects the intonation and the general tone color.

Iran has traditionally been considered the home of the spike fiddle *(rebab),* which is also known as the "poet's fiddle" or *assha'ir.* The fiddle of North Africa, known as a *rbab,* is almost identical in construction and function to the fiddle of Iran. Both are equipped with two strings. Note also the similarity in their names.

six pairs of strings, some made of gut and some of wire. Although the *'ud* is not popularly played among the non-Islamic

[1] For very good examples of *'ud* music, play the UNESCO Collection recording *Tunisia,* side one, band 4, solo for fretted *'ud,* and band 5, solo for unfretted *'ud.*

The Islamized Tuaregs of the Sahara have, however, a one-stringed fiddle called *amzhad* (or *imzhad*), which is used to accompany songs of love.

Fiddles are often found in the hands of professional performers. The one-stringed Ethiopian fiddle, the *masinKo*,*

is exclusively played by the *azmari*, poet-musicians. Commenting on these musicians, Mondon-Vidailhet wrote the following:

> One would never imagine that the players could draw such resonances from such a primitive instrument, but nevertheless some of them possess real virtuosity. They make use of position-work and even produce harmonics. What is even stranger is that they resort to the vibrato, to bring variety into their melodies, in the same way as do our violinists and cellists. As for the tablature, it approximates more to the viola than to the violin or cello.[2]

Traditionally, an Ethiopian vocal performance begins with an instrumental introduction. The solo *masinKo* covers the tones within the proper melodic mode and assures the singer of the establishment of the proper *Kignit* (modal tuning) within the vocalist's range. The *masinKo* also alternates with the voice, playing one whole cycle of the song alone after the voice. This enables the singer to rest, particularly in an extended performance. It also affords time to ponder over circumstances and think up impromptu verses. There are times when the *masinKo* part interplays with the vocal melody imitatively. The instrumental interludes between verses and phrases also serve to heighten the emotional content.[3]

The fiddle of the neighboring Sudan is similar to the Ethiopian *masinKo* in

---

*The glottalized consonant sounds of the Amharic language—*K* and *C*—are indicated by capital letters; they do not have English equivalents. To sound *K*, the tongue is formed as *k* but exploded. To sound *C*, the tongue is formed like *ch* in *church* but

exploded. For additional information, see Ashenafi Kebede's *The Music of Ethiopia*, pp. 270–2.

[2]Read Mondon-Vidailhet's article "La Musique éthiopienne." In this quotation, he uses the term *tablature* to mean "timbre."

[3]For a sound example of fiddle music, play *The Music of Ethiopia: Azmari Music of the Amharas*, side one, band 5.

Figure 9.3. MasinKo player. Photo by A. Kebede. All rights reserved, Ashenafi Kebede Collection.

both construction and musical function. It is also historically related. It is believed that the instrument came from South Arabia with the Guhaina Arabs who came to Sudan via Ethiopia. Known as *umkiki*, the fiddle is predominantly found among the southern Kordufan and Darfur traditions of Sudan. Here again, the forces of Islam are deep-rooted, and the instrument is used to accompany improvised verses set to melodies sung homophonically by specialized craftsmen and women; love, praise, satire, and particularly patriotism are the most common themes of the texts.

In West Africa, the *griots*, the professional musicians of the Islamized regions, play a one-stringed fiddle called a *godie* that is especially popular among the Hausa people. The *godie* is constructed and played much like the Ethiopian and Sudanese fiddles.

Lyres

Lyres are structurally distinguished from other chordophones in the following ways: Two wooden sideposts emerge from a sound resonator; a crossbar or yoke connects the posts on the top opposite the resonator; the strings, stretched from the crossbar down to the bottom of the resonator, always run parallel to the face of the resonator. There are two types of lyres, *bowl lyre* and *box lyres*. The term *bowl lyre* refers to the lyre type with circular- or bowl-shaped resonator, and *box lyre* to the type with square-, rectangular-, or box-shaped res-

onator. Lyres are found in many of the northeast African, Near Eastern, and Mediterranean cultures. For example, it is known as *kinnor* in Hebrew, *kinnara* in Arabic, *ginera* in old Egyptian, and *lyra* in Greek.

Historically, Egyptian paintings of about 2000 B.C. show Semitic nomads with lyres. It is not certain, however, how much Egyptians exerted their influence on Asian and Mediterranean musical cultures. Types of box lyres are found in many parts of western Asia. The construction of the soundbox of these Asiatic

Figure 9.4. Sudanese lyres and players at the Khartoum Archive.
Photo by A. Kebede. All rights reserved, Ashenafi Kebede Collection.

lyres is square, like the ancient Greek *kithara*. The Hebrew lyres were small, with bowl-shaped resonators.

Lyres are widely distributed in most of the northeastern and eastern African cultures. Uganda is famed for its large variety of bowl lyres. Ugandan lyres generally use a tuning bulge on the yoke to tune the gut strings. Ethiopian lyres, unlike the Ugandan, have tuning twigs or sticks. In the Sudan, tradition indicates that the lyre comes from Arabian sources. On the other hand, the rock paintings and frescoes of earlier times in Sudan show ritual dances and musicians playing the harp or lyre; the frescoes and rock paintings that still survive belong to

the dominant Sudanese kingdoms of Nubia and Merewetiks. Mahi Ismail, formerly of the School of Music, Dance, and Drama in Sudan, believes that it was the Merewetiks who carried the lyre from Arabia to Africa as far south as Ethiopia.[4] All Sudanese lyres have bowl-shaped resonators. They are played by stopping the five or six strings with the fingers of one hand while strumming them with plectra of leather with the other hand. A

[4]Personal communication with Mahi Ismail, former director of the Institute of Music, Dance, and Drama in Khartoum, Sudan. Also see his article "Les Traditions musicales du Soudan." In addition, I have confirmed the accuracy of the information during my 1979 mission as a UNESCO consultant to the government of Sudan.

similar technique is applied in playing Ethiopian lyres.[5]

Ethiopia is the only country where the box lyre *(begena)* is found today. Wood from eucalyptus or juniper trees is ordinarily used in making the frame of the soundbox. It is then covered by parchment made of oxhide. The box is sometimes made of a hollowed-out piece of wood of appropriate circumference and depth. Neither of the Ethiopian lyres—the bowl lyre *(krar)* and the box lyre *(begena)*—has rattles on its surface as some of the other African lyres do, such as those in Uganda and Zaire. Most lyres use a bridge that stands on the face of the resonator. The bridge has slots equal to the number of the strings, and its purpose is to lift the strings off the face of the resonator so each string can vibrate freely and produce clear tones. One end of each string is tied to the loop on the sound resonator and the other end around the yoke with the tuning twigs or pegs. These pegs are turned to tighten the strings to the required pitches.

Traditionally, the strings of the *begena* were made of ox or cow gut. Most African housewives are familiar with the ways of preparing gut strings, as they often need and use it for the cotton bow. The animal is normally butchered at home for meat. The useful part of the intestines is cleaned, scrubbed, and carefully stretched to dry. Depending on the required length and thickness, two or more single threads may be wound together to make one string; just one gut is used to make a string. The taller the instrument, the lower its tones and the thicker the strings.

[5]Ashenafi Kebede, "The Bowl-Lyre of Northeast Africa," pp. 381–90.

The soundbox is covered by parchment made out of the hide. After the animal is butchered, the hide is carefully separated from the meat using a sharp, pointed long knife. Simple as it may sound, it actually requires training and practice to perform this rather tedious operation of removing the hide without any bruises. The skin alone is then stretched and the hair is closely shaved before it dries. While shaving, it is most important again that no cuts at all be made in the skin, as otherwise the skin will not serve the intended purpose of covering the *begena* soundbox.

The most important stage of the work (which requires the musical artistic ear and the accompanying specialized skill of the *begena* maker) includes selecting and preparing the wood for the frame of the soundbox, the side arms, the yoke or crossbar, the bridge, and the pegs. Juniper is preferred as it is better able to resist weather changes.

Lyres of varying sizes and with different numbers of strings are also found in Kenya: large, with twelve strings *(obukano);* medium, with eight strings *(litungu);* and small, with five strings *(kibugander* or *kibugandet)*. It is important to note that East Africa is truly the home of lyres, where they are actively utilized in music performances; there are no lyres in West Africa.

Lyres provide in addition, an excellent means for the reconstruction of culture history and the study of musical migration and distribution around the Mediterranean cultures of Africa, the Near East, and Europe.

Krar Music: Tuning and Performance

Aside from a few documented statements of a general nature concerning *krar* music, the system of tuning and the techniques employed in *krar* performance have not been seriously studied. The remarks made by some writers are often too general to be of any informative value. For example, Curt Sachs supposes that

> the Ethiopian lyre *kerar* has preserved the ancient Greek, or even Mediterranean, accordatura. Indeed, modern Ethiopia, the only country with two lyres besides ancient Greece, tunes them in a different arrangement, though to the same pentatonic scale.[6]

Another musicologist, Alain Daniélou, detects connections between the Greek *lyra* and the Ethiopian *krar*, particularly in the general sound quality and the tuning approaches. The *krar* music, Daniélou writes,

Figure 9.5. Ethiopian krar player. Photo by A. Kebede. All rights reserved, Ashenafi Kebede Collection.

appears to belong to the great civilization which spread in the Mediterranean world before its wanton destruction of the Arabs and the Europeans. [The *krar* music] appears the nearest thing I have ever heard to ancient Greek music and the *krar* itself appears tuned exactly like the ancient lyra.[7]

Frankly, these remarks add very little, if anything, to our knowledge of the system of *krar* tuning or *krar* music. In fact, it may be presumptuous for us to discuss the similarities between the sound quality, tuning and performance styles of Ethiopian and Greek lyres. The sound forms of ancient Greek music obviously have not been recorded and are unknown

Figure 9.6. yefikir ketaima krar tuning.

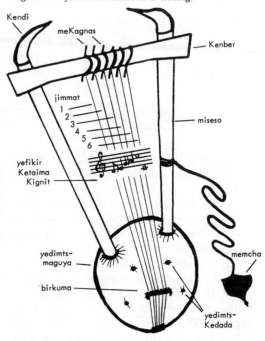

[6]Curt Sachs, *The History of Musical Instruments*, p. 134.

[7]Personal communication with Alain Daniélou.

Figure 9.7. *Krar music* yefikir ketaima.

to anyone. On the other hand, *krar* music is the living music of contemporary Ethiopia.

The *krar* is always tuned to a pentatonic scale. The performer tunes his instrument using the method of alternation. Tuning starts with the highest-pitched string, the fifth. This fifth string must be tuned in a manner that would allow the singer to reproduce it vocally without a strain. As shown in Figure 9.6., the fifth string is tuned to C. The third string is next tuned to G, a perfect fourth below high C. Then the fourth string is

tuned to A♭, a major third below high C or a minor second above G. The six strings of the *krar* are tuned within a tonal range of an octave. Consequently, the remaining three strings are easily tuned using the following procedure. The sixth string of the *krar* is tuned to low C, an octave below high C. Note that the fifth and sixth strings are always tuned an octave apart. Then the player tunes the first string to D, a perfect fourth below G. Last, the second string is tuned to E♭, a major third below G or a fourth below A♭. This is one of many pentatonic melodic modes called *yefikir ketaima* that consists of low C, D, E♭, G, and high C.

Two main techniques are employed in the performance of *krar* music.

All the strings can be strummed by a leather plectrum about two inches above the bridge. The five fingers of the left hand are positioned behind the six strings about three inches below the yoke. The thumb, placed between the first and second strings, is used to damp both. Each of the remaining four fingers is placed behind one string. In this performance technique, the player leaves the string with the desired pitch open to vibrate freely by lifting the appropriate finger of the left hand while simultaneously damping the remaining five strings with the other four fingers. In this *strumming technique* the desired melodic progressions are created.

The second technique utilizes string plucking with the bare fingers of the left hand. Most of the master performers use this *plucking technique*, which enables them to execute highly ornamented melodic passages based on a vocal melody.[8] (See Figure 9.7.)

Zithers

A *zither* may be simply defined as an instrument with horizontal strings that are the same length as its soundboard. (Outside Africa, it is found in the greatest numbers in China, Korea, and Japan.)

A zither that has gained recognition as an important instrument of virtuosity is the *qanun*. It has existed with up to 105 strings. In North Africa, it is played with picks that are worn on the index fingers. The closely related *santur* of Iran, on the other hand, is played with two beaters. This dulcimer is of interest because it is an ancestor of such Western instruments as the clavichord and the piano.

In the Malagasy Republic (Madagascar), there exist two interesting zither types. The *valiha,* a tube zither, is made of bamboo and twelve to twenty wire strings. The other type, *jejo vaotano,* is a stick zither with four to twelve strings. According to Grame, both zither types were brought to the island by a Malayan people, the Hovas, who moved there in the fifteenth century. However, the performance style and musical content—such as frequent use of diatonic scales and parallel thirds—have become distinctively African.[9]

Other popular types indigenous to the societies of sub-Saharan Africa include monochord (one-string), raft, bow, and trough zithers. In most of these instruments, the strings are made of bark strips or strands held away from the frame with a bridge; they are cut along the lengths of the stick in such ways that the strands remain attached to it at both ends. Sometimes resonators are attached at different locations; they are used for purposes of sound amplification; in other words, they help the instrument sound

[8]For detailed information, read Kebede's "The Bowl-Lyre of Northeast Africa," pp. 379–395.
[9]Theodore C. Grame, "Bamboo and Music," pp. 142–149.

louder. The *mvet* of Cameroon has two resonators attached to each end. In the case of the bow zither, only one resonator is located at the center. These resonators are made of gourd. Such sound amplification devices are not always attached to the instrument, nor are they made from gourds. For example, *valiha* performers place the end of their instruments on any available empty can when they desire to play loud.[10]

Harps

In *harps*, the strings run perpendicular to the soundboard. (This is unlike lyres and zithers, which have strings that lie parallel.)

Popular among blind musicians, the Egyptian harp, *bin't*, was played by both men and women. The existence of

Figure 9.8. A harp popularly found in sub-Saharan Africa. Photo by Harry Knight, Exton Studio. Armer Collection of Nigerian Artifacts. © Copyright 1980 FSU Center for Black Culture. Used by permission of FSU Center for Black Culture.

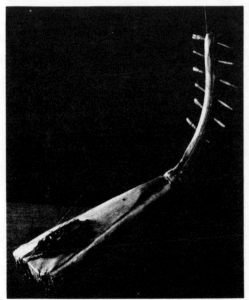

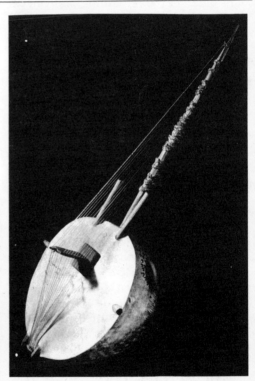

Figure 9.9. Gambian kora. Gift of Fayee Ephraim Joiner. Ashenafi Kebede Collection. Copyright 1980 FSU Center for Black Culture. Used by permission of FSU Center for Black Culture.

this instrument today in India (known as *bin* in Hindi and *vina* in Sanskrit) is

[10]Listen to *Madagascar. Valiha.*

etymologically indicative of strong African influence on Asia. There is no doubt that the modern European harp is derived from the Mesopotamian standing harp, documented as early as 3000 B.C.

In Sudan, the harp has a gourd resonator covered by sheep or goat skin.

The *kora* is undoubtedly one of the most beautiful stringed instruments of sub-Saharan Africa. Structurally, it is a combination of a lute and a harp. Like a lute, the *kora* neck extends all the way through the soundbox or the resonator. Unlike the lute, the (usually)twenty-one strings of the *kora* are not arranged to cross the bridge parallel to the resonator but are stretched in two rows, one on each side of the bridge, perpendicular to the face of the soundbox. Each string is tied to a movable hide ring around the neck that serves as a tuning bulge; consequently, the entire neck of the *kora* is a tuning apparatus. Since the performer faces the bridge when playing, the sound hole is located on the back of the instrument closer to the audience. Like a harp, each string is tuned to only one tone. The *kora* is played with the thumb and forefinger of each hand; the other fingers are used to keep the instrument in a vertical position. Because of the complexity involved in the making and playing of such a sophisticated instrument, the *kora* is most often found in the hands of the

Figure 9.10. The position in which the kora is played.
Photograph by Eliot Elisofon. Museum of African Art, Smithsonian Institution,
Eliot Elisofon Archives. Used by permission.

professional musician. This applies to Gambia and Guinea, for example, where the *kora* is popular.

Kora music is currently gaining some popularity in the United States. Discussing encounters with *griots* who played the instrument (at the Alternative Center for International Arts), one American reviewer wrote:

> Even more impressive than the wealth of musical traditions that can be found around the world is our ignorance of so many of them. Every time I begin to feel I am finally gaining a general awareness of at least the major categories of the world's music, I come across another one.[11]

It is true that *kora* players often attain levels of virtuosity that can be compared with those of other instrumental traditions in the world. Though short vocal refrains are sung to signal a change in theme and to end an improvisational section, *kora* music is generally instrumental. When performing in a duo, one player establishes and maintains intricate ostinato cycles, while the other embroiders elaborately long melodies. The *kora* performers use staccato chording, cross-rhythms, and spellbinding improvisations that display superior technical and artistic proficiency.

Al Haji Bai Konte and his son Dembo Konte, both *griots* from Gambia, are among the numerous musicians popularizing African music in the United States. As another American reviewer indicated, *kora* music is a remarkable tradition that could become as popular in the Western world as Indian music if it were better known.[12]

Basic Terms

If you aren't sure what each of the following terms means, look back at the text, where they appear in italic type. Additional information about some of them may also be found by checking the index.

chordophones	kithara
lutes	begena
plucked lutes	krar
'ud	obukano
rebab	litungu
assha'ir	kibugander
rbab	kibugandet

amzhad	kerar
imzhad	yefikir ketaima
masinKo	strumming
azmari	technique
Kignit	plucking technique
umkiki	zither
griots	qanun
godie	santur
bowl lyre	valiha
box lyre	jejo vaotano
kinnor	mvet
kinnara	harp
ginera	bin't
lyra	kora

[11]Tom Johnson, "Encounters with Griots."

[12]Robert Palmer, "Music: Bai Konte Plays on Harp of West Africa."

Bibliography

GRAME, THEODORE C., "Bamboo and Music: A New Approach to Organology," *Readings in Ethnomusicology*, ed. David P. McAllester. New York: Johnson Reprint Corp., 1971, pp. 142–149.

ISMAIL, MAHI, "Musical Traditions in the Sudan," *African Music*, pp. 94–98. (This is the English translation of the following listed work.)

——, "Les Traditions musicales du Soudan," *La Revue Musicale* (UNESCO, Paris) 288–289 (1972):87–93.

JOHNSON, TOM, "Encounters with Griots," *The Village Voice*, July 9, 1979, p. 58.

KEBEDE, ASHENAFI, "The Bowl-Lyre of Northeast Africa. *Krar:* The Devil's Instrument," *Ethnomusicology* 21 (3—1977):379–395.

KING, ANTHONY, "The Construction and Tuning of the *Kora*," *African Language Studies* 13 (1972):133–136.

MONDON-VIDAILHET, F.M.C., "La musique 'ethiopienne," *Encyclopédie de la musique et dictionnaire du conservatoire* (part one), ed. A. Lavignac and L. de la Laurencie. Paris: C. Delagrave, 1922, pp. 3179–96.

PALMER, ROBERT, "Music: Bai Konte Plays on Harp of West Africa," *The New York Times*, June 11, 1979, p. 15.

SACHS, CURT, *The History of Musical Instruments*. New York: W.W. Norton & Co., 1940.

SPECTOR, JOHANNA, "Classical 'Ud Music in Egypt with Special Reference to Maqamat," *Ethnomusicology* 14(2—1970):243–257.

VARNUM, JOHN P.,– The *Obokano* of the Gusii: A Bowl Lyre of East Africa," *Ethnomusicology* 15(2—1971):242–248.

Discography

Cordes anciennes. Produced by the Ministry of Information of Mali. Barenreiter BM 30 L 2506.

Kora manding: Mandinka Music of The Gambia. Recording and commentary by Roderic Knight. Ethnodisc ER 12102. (This record comes with forty-four pages of descriptive notes, songs, texts, etc.)

Madagascar. Valiha. Ocora OCR 18.

The Music of Africa Series. Strings. Hugh Tracey. No. 27. GALP 1322.

The Music of Ethiopia: Azmari Music of the Amharas. Recordings and notes by Ashenafi Kebede. Anthology Records AST-6000.

Musique du Burundi. Recording and commentary by Michel Vuylsteke. Ocora OCR 40. (Play side two, band 4 for an example of the *inanga*, or trough zither, and side one, band 5 for the *umuduri*, or musical bow.

Musique centrafricaine. Recording and commentary by Charles Duvelle. Ocora OCR 43. (This record includes one interesting example of a harp-zither—*bogongo*—played by a Pygmy vocalist.)

Tunisia. Recording and commentary by Alain Daniélou. UNESCO Collection. BM 30 L 2008.

III

MUSIC AND OTHER ASPECTS OF AFRICAN CULTURE

10 Legend, Magic, Myth, and Symbolism

The Origins of Music

Many societies around the world trace the origins of their music to animals, supernatural sources, or individual composers. This is also true in many African traditions. The Ashanti, for example, identify the source of their music to a bird:

> The *kokokyinaka* is a beautiful dark bird that frequents the forest … Its call is not unlike the notes of the drums. It is every drummer's totem, they claim kinship with it and would not eat or kill it. Its call is something like kro kro kro kro ko kyini kyini kyini kro kyini ka ka ka kyini kyini kyini kyini ka. The Ashanti say it taught them to drum.[1]

Imitation of bird calls seems to be quite popular among many African cultures. In Sierra Leone, a small boy is credited with the introduction of *balanji* xylophone music after he fashioned it in imitation of birdsong.

> According to stories handed over to succeeding generations by word of mouth, "balanji" music was introduced by a small boy of about ten years of age. It is said that while he was going to his father's farm early in the morning, he heard a little bird whistling in the woods, and, greatly impressed by the melodious voice of the bird … he stopped and listened to a song … He went on his way, cut some sticks and shaped them flat. He cut another two sticks, and, after arranging the former on his lap, he began to strike them with the latter … This lad succeeded in playing the song which he picked up from the mouth of the bird. This song is known and played by every "balanji" player.[2]

[1]Alan P. Merriam, *The Anthropology of Music*, p. 75. [2]*Ibid.*, p. 65.

In the mythologies and folklores of many cultures, music came into being through some association with godly figures. In Egypt, the gods were closely identified with music. The god *Thoth* was the inventor of music; the dwarf *Bes* was the lord of music and dancing. Most religious rituals were accompanied by music, and the Egyptians' attribution of supernatural powers to music was mirrored by many Mediterranean cultures, especially the Greeks.

The performer of music is also associated with supernatural powers. In Morocco, Tunisia, and western Sudan, the professional musicians—the *essawa*, *gnawa*, and *griots*—often perform healing ceremonials. Consequently the performance of music to cure the sick has cast the performers in a highly important role in these societies. Though these players are considered of low caste, their power through music is assuredly recognized in these Islamized regions.

In West Africa, among the Ashanti, people believe "the man in the moon" to be a drummer. According to Nketia:

> The drummer of the talking drums is called the Creator's Drummer....He is closest to the spirit of the ancestor chiefs whom he addresses...The creator's drummer is close to Nature....He exercises to the spirit of the objects of creation from whom the components of his drum are obtained....He also calls on the Supreme Being, to lesser gods, witches, Ancestor drummers ... capable of interfering with his work or his well-being... [3]

Many other West African communities have specialized music dedicated to and named after diverse deities. The Yoruba, the Dahomeans, and the Ewe of Togo and southern Ghana worship *Afa*, the god of divination. Afa music largely consists of drumming, singing, and dancing. And according to Ladzekpo, Yewe music, named after *Yewe*, the god of thunder and lightning, is considered to be one of the most developed forms of sacred music in Anlo. [4]

In Ethiopian culture, where the Christian Church plays a dominant role, creativity is conceived to be the realm of God alone. In fact, the common word for God, *Fetari*, means "the Creator." The artists, the human agents, are only instruments through whom the miracles of art are divinely communicated: they are mediums between the Creator and the people for whom the work is presented. In another area, among the Basongye of the Congo, there is no individual creation. Musical creativity comes directly from their god *Efile Mukulu*, who is nonhuman. However, the performance of music is in all cases carried out by human beings.

It is clear why music is closely related to religion in almost all African cultures. Music helps us to pass into other realms of consciousness. The heightened feeling enhanced by musical experience is aligned with spirituality and the other world— "the world in which things are no longer subject to time and space." [5] David McAllester, one of the founders of the Society of Ethnomusicology, has cited music as one of the two "peak experiences" most important in human lives; the other is, of course, sex. [6]

Correlation of music and its instru-

---

[3] J.H.K. Nketia, "The Role of the Drummer in Akan Society," p. 36.

[4] Alfred K. and Kobla Ladzekpo, "Anlo Ewe Music in Anyako, Volta Region, Ghana," pp. 218–9.
[5] John Blacking, *How Musical Is Man?*, p. 51.
[6] David P. McAllester, "Some Thoughts on Universals in World Music," p. 380.

ments with myth, magic, symbolism, and supernatural powers is a phenomenon observed in most cultures of the world, East and West. Though European ethnomusicologists of the past decades (especially Curt Sachs and Jaap Kunst) have often exaggerated its prevalence in non-Western cultures, it is by no means limited to the societies of Africa and Asia.

European traditions also have it in great abundance. According to Greek mythology, for example, music had a divine origin; gods and demigods—*Apollo, Amphion, Orpheus*, and others— were credited with its invention. In fact, the word *music* is derived from *Muse*, one of the nine Greek goddesses who presided over the arts. As an instrument and invention of gods, music assumed a magical power. We discover in the myth of the Thracian Orpheus that he was able to control the laws of nature by his lyre playing; among other things, he rescued his dead wife from Hades. Philosophers, such as Aristotle and Plato, believed that afflictions of the body (both physical and mental) could be healed by music. Plato, like Confucius in China a century before him, was convinced that musical change, either in intonation, form, or style, could cause social change; consequently, governments must consider the importance of music in the maintenance of healthy societies. Fascinating accounts found in the Old Testament provide us with excellent examples of the powers of music. These include David's curing Saul's madness by playing the lyre, the trumpet blasts that brought the walls of Jericho tumbling down, and many others. In addition, music was directly associated with the fine arts in general, as the primal source of beauty and truth.

Basic Terms

If you cannot identify the terms or names that follow, look back at the text, where they appear in italic type. Additional information about some of them may also be found by checking the index.

kokokyinaka	Yewe
balanji	Fetari
Thoth	Efile Mukulu
Bes	Apollo
essawa	Amphion
gnawa	Orpheus
griots	Muse
Afa	

Bibliography

BLACKING, JOHN, *How Musical Is Man?*, Seattle: University of Washington Press, 1973.

LADZEKPO, ALFRED K. and KOBLA, "Anlo Ewe Music in Anyako, Volta Region, Ghana," *Musics of Many Cultures*, ed. Elizabeth May. Los Angeles: University of California Press, 1980, pp. 216–231.

MCALLESTER, DAVID P., "Some Thoughts on Universals in World Music," *Ethnomusicology* 15(3—1971):379–380.

MERRIAM, ALAN P., *The Anthropology of Music*, Evanston, Illinois: Northwestern University Press, 1964.

NKETIA, J.H. KWABENA, "The Role of the Drummer in Akan Society," *African Music* 1(1954):34–43.

11 Symbolism in Musical Instruments

Many instruments have symbolic associations with animate and inanimate objects. Consequently, it is important to know the native symbolisms, personifications, and mythological or magical connotations that Africans attribute to them.

The human body is undoubtedly the oldest of all musical instruments. Singing, handclapping, footstamping on sound-producing objects, chestbeating to accompany funeral chants, and other similar activities predate the invention and use of instruments made of materials that nature provides, such as flutes, fiddles, skin-covered wooden drums, sticks, and metal bells. Sticks and rattles served as extensions of the human body. Instruments were initially used by shamans, healers, and ethnic religious leaders; they were used in the attainment of magical and religious power more than for purely musical purposes. Instrumental

music thus came from social and extra-musical sources.

Curt Sachs thinks that innumerable instruments of the non-European world that we study today developed from sources interrelated with magic and religion. Some rhythmic instruments developed for the accompaniment of ritualistic dance; these were worn on the wrist, waist, ankle, or head.

In Egyptian mythology the cult of *Hathor*, goddess of love, was embodied in the sistrum. Even the columns of her temple were conceived as colossal sistra. Many wall paintings in tombs and other material evidence indicate that the instrument was undoubtedly associated with and used by women. The four jingling metal bars on the sistrum are linked with the elements of nature: fire, water, air, and earth. In most of the cults, the sistrum was identified with votive power. We have already mentioned that

West African tribes—the Boule and M'Wan, for example—use it in initiation rites for the excision of girls; it is played by women, and sometimes by girls. On the other hand, in Ethiopia the sistra are strictly religious instruments played only by male deacons and priests to accompany sacred chants. In this case, close relationships exist between Ethiopian and Jewish practices in the use of the sistrum; in both cultures, they are played by male priests.

Metallic idiophones had a historical role of protecting the bearer against evil spirits. In the North African cultures of Egypt and Tunisia, for example, beautiful women, children, and even attractive horses, cows, and calves are seen with bells and jingles dangling on their necks. The purpose of wearing them is neither musical nor decorative: it is to protect them from the evil eye. In addition, jingles are used in the rites of initiation and circumcision and as protection against the bite of serpents. (The extramusical protective role of instruments is a phenomenon also seriously practiced in European cultures. In A.D. 900, for example, Pope John IX ordered that bells be used in the Catholic Church as a defense against thunder and lightning.) It is edifying to study how musical instruments serve religious and symbolic roles in society.

In all Orthodox Christian churches, including the Ethiopian and Egyptian churches, the censers and silver pyxes are provided with jingles. Even Biblical references indicate that Hebraic priests wore metallic jingles on their robes upon entering sacred places such as the Holy of Holies. This is still practiced in many Christian and Jewish communities, including those found today in oriental Africa, such as the black Jews of Ethiopia and the Coptic Christians of Egypt.

Idiophones are often used in the sphere of sacred music and other nonmusical semireligious activities. The spherical jingle, which is popularly found throughout oriental Africa, is known under onomatopoetic names in Afro-Semitic languages: *al-gulgul, shkelkil* (Egyptian), *al-galag* (Sudan), and *quachil* (Ethiopia). The bell with clapper is symbolic of a male baby.

In sub-Saharan Africa, rattles are part of the native healer's equipment; they are used to ward off evil spirits. Vessel rattles are sometimes used by the rainmakers. Many traditions have prescriptions in regard to ownership of musical instruments, their symbolism, and which sex should play them. An instrument such as the Nigerian net rattle, *shekere*, is often made for a specific musician. It is never lent. Only a son may inherit it, provided that he is a professional musician. The gourd used in making rattles is symbolic of fertility; it always grows near a body of water, and its general shape is reminiscent of a woman's womb.

Seasonal changes are marked by music and musical instruments. In northern Togo, for example, the sound of stone chimes marks the end of the rainy season; it also announces the feast of the millet harvest (millet is an important national food in many African countries). Stone chimes, or lithophones, are popularly used in Nigeria and Cameroon, where their sound is incorporated into magic rituals, spiritual communications, and initiation rites.

Musical instruments possess sexual symbolism according to most traditions. "Curt Sachs would probably say 'almost all traditions,'" Titcomb tells me. "He used to talk about it even in connection with the European traditions."[1] For example, among the Kiganda of Uganda, the xylophone of sixteen keys reflects male-female symbolism in three groups: the high keys (1–6) are considered girlish, the middle keys (7–11) womanly, and the low keys (12–16) manly. This tradition also associates dance with the xylophone. The slit-drum is symbolic of femininity.

Drums are often symbolic of high office in most African cultures. The Hausa drum of Nigeria called *taushi* is a symbol of aristocratic status; it is a cone-shaped single-membrane drum played by court musicians. The *atumpan*, the master drum of the Ashanti, is another example of a membranophone that is actively associated with high office. The installation of a new chief requires the building of a new set of drums to be played on the day of his inauguration. The drum, in addition, is considered a disperser of evil spirits; when a person dies, it is played night and day to keep witches away until the corpse is buried. The drumstick is a phallic symbol. A drum itself is widely regarded as a uterine symbol.

Some tribes, like the Akan, have the idea that spirits inhabit material objects. For example, the cedar is supposed to be the abode of a spirit, and rites are performed before cutting down the tree to carve drums. The spirit is propitiated before using the wood. The drummer comes to be identified with the spirit too. Thus the Akan drummer of the *atumpan* is called *Tweneboa Kodua; Tweneboa* is

Figure 11.1. Ghanaian drum with symbols carved on its body. Photograph by Eliot Elisofon. Museum of African Art, Smithsonian Institution, Eliot Elisofon Archives. Used by permission.

the name both of the cedar tree and the spirit. Some ceremonies begin by invoking the spirit Tweneboa, and sometimes the drums are consecrated. Note how the symbolic attributes assigned to the *atumpan* vary between the Akan and the Ashanti, both of Ghana.

Especially in polytheistic Africa, drums are widely used for religious ceremonies and are appropriate for the worship of gods. When employed for religious purposes, drums are frequently considered sacred and are not used for anything else. Moreoever, the drums for one god cannot be employed for another. The colors of religious drums usually match the colors of other ritual objects for purposes of identification.

[1] Professor Caldwell Titcomb, Brandeis University. Personal communications.

Among the Watutsi of eastern Africa, the drum symbolizes royalty. In fact, the king's permission is traditionally required to play a battery of drums. A drum ensemble is employed only on important social and religious occasions.

In Tanzania, a chief's death is announced by the sound of drums. His past rank and important status can be recognized by the number of drums at his funeral. A funeral is, of course, one kind of religious ritual.

Throughout the world, religious and extramusical symbolism is attributed to the instruments of the aerophone class. In ancient Egypt, "flutes are first recorded on a prehistoric slate from Hieraconpolis (fourth millennium B.C.) on which a disguised hunter plays a flute to allure the game."[2] Priests in many parts of Asia and Africa play a bamboo flute for purposes of meditation; shepherds play it to suspend time; soldiers play it to soothe tension; and, for lovers, the sound of the flute enhances romance.

In most cultures, the flute is associated with love, pastoral music, phallus, and wind. It is symbolic of fertility, life, rebirth, and procreation. It is an instrument used for betrothals, courtship, weddings, circumcision, fertility, healing initiation, and sacrificial rites. As a talisman for new life, it is sometimes buried with the dead.[3]

The musicians of Morocco and Tunisia still play on the oboe-type *zorna* or *zurna*) to charm a basketful of snakes. The same practice is a common spectacle in the marketplaces of India, where the musician also uses a related double-reed called *surnay* among Hindus and *nagasvaram* in the Carnatic.)

Myths point to the Nile River as the area of origin of the lyre type of instruments. Mercury is supposed to have devised the lyre when one day he found a dried-out tortoise on the banks of the Nile. On the other hand, historical documents attest that lyres played a great role in Sumerian ceremonies before 2700 B.C.

The Hebrew lyres resemble the lyres of the Nile area, particularly those found in Ethiopia. The Hebrew lyres were small and triangular, had circular soundboxes, and were held in a slanting position. The strings were made of sheep gut. It is interesting to note some functional similarities between the Hebrew lyre and the Ethiopian *krar*. It is believed that during their Babylonian exile, the Jews suspended the use of the instrument because it produced "gay" sounds.

> By the rivers of Babylon,
> There we sat down, yea, we wept,
> When we remembered Zion.
> Upon the willows in the midst thereof
> We hanged up our harps.[4]

And according to Sachs:

> The kinnor was gay, and when the prophets admonished the people they threatened that the kinnor, symbol of joy and happiness, would be silenced unless the people desisted from sin. Instruments still were bound to well-defined occasions and modes.[5]

---

[2]Curt Sachs, *The History of Musical Instruments*, p. 90.

[3]Maria Leach, ed., *Standard Dictionary of Folklore, Mythology, and Legend*, pp. 395–397.

[4]Psalm 137.

[5]Sachs, p. 108.

Basic Terms

If you cannot identify the terms or names that follow, look back at the text, where they appear in italic type. Additional information about some of them may also be found by checking the index.

Hathor	atumpan
al-gulgul	Tweneboa Kodua
shkelkil	tweneboa
al-galag	zorna
quachil	zurna
shekere	surnay
taushi	nagasvaram

Bibliography

KEBEDE, ASHENAFI, "The Bowl-Lyre of Northeast Africa. *Krar:* The Devil's Instrument," *Ethnomusicology* 21(3—1977):379–395.

LEACH, MARIA, ed., *Standard Dictionary of Folklore, Mythology, and Legend.* New York: Funk & Wagnalls, 1972.

SACHS, CURT, *The History of Musical Instruments.* New York: W.W. Norton & Co., 1940.

12 Dance and Music

Dance is a physical phenomenon that is culturally patterned. Different cultures demonstrate diversity in their movements. The styles of dance also differ according to sex, age, social status, profession, nationality, and ethnic membership. In fact, societies differentiate their members from those of other cultures by the way they dance. Dance is important for joy and sorrow, war and peace.

Dance can symbolize ideas and activities, such as religious beliefs and social activities. There are *ritual dances* only for religious occasions. As an important part of the traditional activities of society, dance is incorporated in religious ceremonials along with music. The religious leaders (priests or priestesses) often perform the leading dance roles. In most of sub-Saharan Africa, dancers wear masks in the celebration of various cults, such as gods and goddesses of the earth, the sea, war, fertility, and the seasons.

The *zar dances* of some of the societies around the Horn of Africa, particularly in Egypt, Ethiopia, and Sudan, are performed by shamans in trance; in other words, through dance, the shaman achieves a self-induced trance in order to communicate with spirits. Incense is often burned; rhythmic music and chanting make up an important part of the *zar* (spirit) dances.

Spirit dances are common in most parts of Africa. The African lifestyle in spirit dances and music has extended itself to the slave areas of the New World—the Caribbean, Venezuela, and eastern Brazil. The *vodou* rite of Haiti consists of remarkable characteristics traced to several West African tribes, the Yoruba predominating; in addition, they have blended European religious beliefs and Catholic saints with the African.* The devotees often perform spirit dances

*The word *vodou* comes from the Ewe *vodu*.

to hypnotic drumbeats; those dancers possessed by a deity perform frenzied and acrobatic movements.

Dance is important in the secular activities of all African societies. These activities include weddings, births, and funerals. As a social activity, dance brings men and women of marriageable age together. *Wedding dances* are performed by both sexes, usually in double files that often meet and separate. Parents and grandparents actively participate in the celebration of marriage. Dance is known to serve the purposes of politics: the authority of a chief is acknowledged through celebrations that feature specialized dances, music, and poetry befitting the occasion.

Dance also provides us with symbolic meaning: women's and men's body movements often differ, thereby helping us make distinctions between male and female roles in a given society. Generally speaking, *male dances* involve greater vigor in performance than *female dances;* they include jumping, kicking, and leaping. This does not imply feminine inferiority; the often horizontal (earthbound) women's tricky turns and pert movements are just as demanding as the men's vertical dances. There are some forms, however, in which both men's and women's movements are similar.

There is no doubt that the act of dancing advances a feeling of belonging and solidarity among the participating group. We have already indicated that there are male dances and female dances. In addition, there are dances based along occupational lines. The professional or occupational life of a community is expressed through dance and music. Organizations of hunters, farmers, woodcutters, and fishermen have their own dances with mimetic move-

ments taken from their occupations— sowing seeds, grinding corn, hunting, and so on.

It is easy to understand why dance in Africa serves as a significant educational tool in advancing the traditional objectives of society. First, it keeps young men and women physically fit. Second, besides keeping them off the streets, it guides them toward occupational or vocational careers. Body control and discipline are mastered through occupational dances. And last, dance inculcates the feeling of togetherness and patriotism among the participants.

Animal dances are often performed to convey the flavor of hunting, to propitiate the soul of the hunted animal, to reflect totemic worship, or to protray pantomime. Dancers mime revered animals, important personages, and ancestors in order to achieve transformation. Men are generally attracted to miming horned animals; women associate themselves with aquatic creatures, such as fish and swans. This is especially true among the Pygmies.

Dance is a form of nonverbal communication. Facial expressions, gestures, and body movements often carry meaningful messages. Clown, trickster, demon, mime, and trance dances are clearly indicated by their titles. Dance clowning is therapeutic, especially in stressful circumstances. Of course, dance often serves as an excellent means of emotional release, physical relaxation, and self-awareness. There are also forms that require exertion and tension.

Traditionally, *war dances* were performed before battle. Owing to growing national consciousness and unity among Africans, the ethnic wars and tribal fights do not occur as much today as before. Many of the traditional war dances are now presented as entertainment in the form of *dance drama*. These war dance dramas use as their theme the historic national or interethnic struggles that have existed in Africa. The war dance and dance drama have thus become both forms of entertainment and sources of historical information. Participating young men learn to coordinate and train their bodies as well as become acquainted with some of the subtle war movements in a form of dance; they learn actual war mentality and real war maneuvers without an actual war. When battles threaten, these men use dance to overcome the initial fear of war and replace it with a feeling of patriotism. In most war dances, skins of lions and tigers are commonly worn by the participants. Shields are held in the left hand, and the right hand may carry a spear or an axe. This applies notably, but not exclusively, to the Chopi and Ethiopian peoples.

The manner of dress varies from region to region. The occasion on which the dance is going to be performed also determines the mode as well as the color of the dancers' costumes. For example, professional mourners throughout Africa clothe themselves in black togas. A black band of cloth around the arm or black feathers worn in a tuft on the head is a sign of mourning. Dancers in some traditions, such as the Yoruba, Hausa, and Fulani, wear robes and cloth wraps when they dance. These dresses function as an extension of their bodies and help to express subtle movements in terms of space. In other traditions, such as the Kambari and the Lopawa of Borgu, dancers prefer minimal wear; the accent is on the body. Quite often the movements of scantily clad dancers are more athletic and vigorous than those of clothed dancers.

Abdominal dances are what the European world calls "belly dances" (often erroneously associated only with the Arabic world). The earliest forms of abdominal dances were, however, performed by dancing girls of ancient Egypt. Consequently, they originated and developed in the Pharaonic palaces and aristocratic courts of Egypt. The Arabs of today consider this so-called "belly dance" Egyptian. In fact, they call it *masri*, or "Egyptian." Of course, only women performed abdominal dances, as they continue to do today throughout North Africa. Today, the belly dance is popularly performed and taught in the Arab world of the Middle East as well as in Europe and America, especially in the United States. It is a form of dance generally performed solo.

Dance Rhythm

It is rhythm that makes dance possible. Rhythm and dance enhance organization and energy. Group dancing following the temporal order of music is one of the healthiest human activities because it allows interpersonal interaction through a unity of artistic purpose. It enables each person to function at his best in the group.

Dancing is the most obvious form of

entertainment to make use of drums. In West Africa, most drummers are also dancers; hence, drummers play important roles in the accompaniment of dance. A dancer is required to pay his respects to the drummers before he begins his performance. He may even present them with a gift. In response, the dancer's name is sounded through the drum language; special praises of the dancer may be played if he is a person with an established reputation. During the performance, the master drummer plays rhythms or makes changes according to the dancer's movements. The drummers have to play as long as the dancer continues to dance; proper behavior, however, requires the dancer not to perform excessively long. The dancer demonstrates his appreciation to the master drummer and his ensemble at the end of the performance usually with a handshake, a bow, or a hug. It must be noted here that master drummers have the privilege of making critical comments to those dancers whose performances exhibit social behavior that does not measure up to traditional standards. This privilege is characteristic, for example, of the Akan people of Ghana.

In some other societies, such as that of the Acholi of Each Africa, each dancer carries a tiny drum in his left hand and a beating stick in his right. All the dancers tap the same rhythmic configurations that accompany their own movements.

Healing and medicinal dances are almost always accompanied by drums. The Wanyamwezi of Tanzania use a special *ngoma,* a long tubular drum about five and a half feet tall and one foot in diameter, that is always beaten with the palms of both hands. The Iteso of Uganda use two drums in their medicinal dances. Both of the drums are beaten by one drummer.

Stamping is one of the most common of dance movements. Rhythmic activity coupled with rhythmic motion is essential for its best execution. Group hip swivels predominate in movements of sub-Saharan African dances. (Outside of Africa, Hawaiian dancers in particular are noted for their group hip shakes.) In Nigeria, among the Yoruba, the legs are used as springs. The knees, hips, and the pelvic area are markedly flexible. The feet are firmly on the ground. The emphasis of movement of the body in general is toward (and not away from) the earth.

The straight torso is often held inclined at an angle toward the earth. It is alternated with an upright position. A close relationship is maintained between the movements of dancers and the rhythm of the accompanying music; since most musicians are also dancers, this relationship is well maintained. In addition, dancers often wear or carry rattles or bells. These idiophones provide percussive accompaniments based on the close relationship between the body movements of the dancers and the rhythms of the music or song.

Leap dances are performed by Africans more than by any other people of the world. The East African Watutsi are best known for their leap dances. The Wanyamwezi and the Wasiba, both of East Africa, also make impressive leaps high into the air. The Gallas of Ethiopia are noted for their group leap dances. Among many tribes in Uganda, the leap is one of the most important dance movements.

African Aesthetics of Music

We have already learned that traditional African music permeates the whole course of human life. In most cases, it is closely associated with the supernatural, gods, or other dieties. It is also used for entertainment as well as for religious worship, healing ceremonials, and rituals. There are educational songs, war songs, insult songs, political songs, therapeutic songs for the emotionally troubled, drinking songs, and so on. The instruments of African music, and the sounds produced, have important symbolic attributes. Some instruments are used both as sound-producing implements as well as protective devices against evil spirits. A few are exclusively used in the rites of initiation and circumcision. Other instruments are played solely for entertainment. Most of Africa's music is integrated with dance and movement. The performer's facial expressions and movements of the body carry messages that enhance the participants' or audience's understanding of the music.

The performance of music and dance in most traditional African societies often provides experiences that involve interrelationships among many senses. This conceptual approach to music has been either misunderstood, distorted, or neglected by most European scholars of African music. Robert Kauffman correctly tells us, for example, that the "tactile aspect of music making has been one of the principal stumbling blocks in Western attempts to understand African music in aesthetic terms."[1] European scholars erroneously associ-ated or often exaggerated the tactile approach to music making as practiced in many sub-Saharan cultures with black eroticism.

Performance of music on instruments such as the mouth bow and *mbira* provide us with good examples of the tactile approach. The performer "hears" music through his skin. In the performance of wind instruments, the vibration of sound is transmitted internally through the bones of the head and translated into pleasurable sensation.

European scholarship has almost always attempted to understand the aesthetic experience of non-Western peoples largely through the development of terminology that accurately explains the word *art*, its function and expression, and even the psychology of creativity in the context of its own European cultural values. This comparative approach has often led to misunderstanding when the scholar-researcher attempts to explain African concepts that do not have European equivalents. There are, however, a few studies by ethnomusicologists concerned by the problem. The Shona verb *kunzwa*, for example, means "to hear," similar to the Ethiopian word *mesmat*. Both of these verbs mean, in addition, "to perceive by touch, sight, or hearing; to understand; to feel." Their meaning is very close to the meaning of aesthetics because they involve all the senses.[2]

Paul Berliner has presented phrases and adjectives that *mbira* players use to describe the relationship among intervals. For example, the lowest register is

---

[1] See Robert Kauffman's "Aesthetics and Shona Music," p. 508.

[2] *Ibid.* See also Ashenafi Kebede's *The Music of Ethiopia*, pp. 48–52.

referred to as *ngwena*, "crocodiles," which is symbolic of old age and "old men's voices"; *nhetete*, the highest register, means "thin keys"; *nhever-angwena* literally means "those who follow the crocodiles," symbolizing "young men's voices"; it refers to the middle register.[3]

In another area, I have explained that the Western conception of tone in terms of high and low does not exist in the Amhara perception of music. Instead,

pitch is described in terms of *KeCin**[*] (thin) and *wofram* (bulky) dimensions. *KeCin* ordinarily refers to persons or things that are slender, tight, tense, and high-strung. The opposite applies to *wofram*. Serious study of intersense modality—the linguistic transfer of descriptions from one sense area to another—as it applies to African culture is an area that will lead to a better understanding of black aesthetics in general.[†]

Basic Terms

If you aren't sure what each of the following terms means, look back at the text, where they appear in italic type. Additional information about some of them may also be found by checking the index.

ritual dances	healing dances
zar dances	medicinal dances
vodou	ngoma
wedding dances	leap dances
male dances	kunzwa
female dances	mesmat
animal dances	ngwena
war dances	nhetete
dance drama	nhever-angwena
abdominal dances	KeCin
masri	wofram

Bibliography

BASCOM, WILLIAM, *Ifa Divination, Communication between Gods and Men in West Africa.* Bloomington: Indiana University Press, 1969

BERLINER, PAUL F., *The Soul of Mbira.* Los Angeles: University of California Press, 1978.

CHERNOFF, JOHN MILLER, *African Rhythm and African Sensibility: Aesthetics and Social Action in African Musical Idioms.* Chicago: University of Chicago Press, 1979.

DANIÉLOU, ALAIN, *Northern Indian Music* London: Barrie and Rockliff, The Cresset Press, 1968.

HERSKOVITZ, MELVILLE J., *Dahomey.* 2 vols. New York: Augustin, 1938.

JOHNSTON, THOMAS F., "Auditory Driving Hallucinogens, and Music-Color Synesthesia in Tsonga Ritual." In *Drugs, rituals and altered states of consciousness,* Edited by Brian M Du Toit. Rotterdam, Netherlands: A.A. Balkema, pp. 217–36, 1977.

KAUFFMAN, ROBERT, "Aesthetics and Shona Music," *Ethnomusicology* 13, no. 3(1969) pp 507–11.

KEBEDE, ASHENAFI, *The Music of Ethiopia* Ann Arbor, Michigan: University Microfilm International, 1971.

---

[3]Paul Berliner, *The Soul of Mbira,* p. 56.

[*]The glottalized consonant sounds of the Amharic language—*K* and *C*—are indicated by capital letters; they do not have English equivalents. To sound *K*, the tongue is formed as in *k* but exploded. To sound *C*, the tongue is formed like *ch* in *church* but exploded. For additional information, see Ashenafi Kebede's *The Music of Ethiopia,* pp. 270–2.

[†]There are fascinating examples of intersense modality in Indian music culture. It is often hard to make distinctions between symbolism and intersense modality. For additional information, read Alain Daniélou's *Northern Indian Music.*

IV MUSIC IN URBAN AFRICAN SOCIETIES

13 Technology and African Music

The communications explosion is a far-reaching development in modern life. It has intensified the extent of aural and visual contact both nationally at the interethnic and externally at the international levels. Human beings of all cultures listen to each other and exchange ideas and creativity through a global dissemination of sound and pictures over the air. Even the Western World, often taken for granted, is not saved from culture change by the impact of the media.

Narayana Menon, a respected Indian musicologist who served as President of the International Music Council (UNESCO), said that some 800 million radio sets with a potential three billion or more listeners—about eighty percent of the population of the world—are tuned to music programs for something like four to five hours a day. This clearly makes radio the most popular and powerful instrument of music education

or miseducation. According to Dr. Mennon, "It can make or unmake musical taste, develop or kill musical activity, make or kill individual reputations on a scale unthinkable in the days before broadcasting."[1]

The establishment of the communications media around the world has played a leading role in accelerating the processes of music change. Most people own or have access to radios. Transistor radio owners are confined to the national stations. Since many African city dwellers own short-wave radios, broadcasts from other countries are popular. For example, radio listeners are familiar with the European BBC, the Voice of America, and other radio stations in neighboring African countries such as Egypt, Sudan, Somalia, and Kenya.

[1]Narayana Menon, "The Influence of the Mass Media on Tomorrow's Public." Unpublished paper read at the World Music Week Conference, Montreal, Canada, 1975.

109

Most African countries run at least two radio stations, each operating on one band or frequency. Broadcasts are directed to the diverse ethnic groups and classes at different times. One of the two Ethiopian radio stations, for example, broadcasts daily news and music in Arabic from 7 to 8 A.M.; this is intended for the Muslim population. The Amharic program is from 8 to 9 A.M. and, as it is the national language, most societies in Ehtiopia tune in. There are programs in English and French for those educated abroad and foreign residents. And since the 1974 takeover of the government by the *Dergue* socialist military regime, programs that are considered "revolutionary" are broadcast in the languages and dialects of the diverse peoples; it is estimated that there are over seventy languages and 300 dialects spoken in Ethiopia.

Some countries, such as Egypt, however, own stations operating on numerous bands. Here radio broadcasting is highly specialized and provides the public with a wide range of programs. In Cairo, for example, one frequency is given over exclusively to a single popular vocalist, Om Kalthoom, while another broadcasts only readings from the Koran. This kind of *generic broadcasting* works best when the society is racially and culturally homogeneous. Muslim societies in many African nations tune in to Egyptian stations (we have already mentioned that Egypt is one of the four centers of Islamic culture).

The popularity of radio in Africa has caused a marked decline in music making, threatening the very existence of the traditional forms of music; the audience for Western popular music has increased dramatically. In most of Africa,

where the music of oral tradition is closely linked to dance, drama, poetry, and other subtle symbolic attributes, culture can be preserved and promoted only through active performance and audience participation, definitely not by passively listening to radios. The problem is aggravated by the relatively short broadcast time given to traditional music. Programs are produced according to consumer demand; audiences often prefer American pop, disco, or urban music.

The cost of television being economically prohibitive for most Africans, its influence is limited to the small circle of wealthy upper-class and foreign-educated middle-class viewers, who are already cosmopolitan by culture.

Western music, particularly black American music, has been widely diffused and made popular by commercial agencies of record and tape corporations. Because of the growth in the number of European-style adult entertainment centers, such as nightclubs, bars, coffee shops, dance saloons, and red-light districts, the demand for and sale of prerecorded tapes of popular music have increased dramatically.

Judging by the sale of records, tapes, and playing equipment, the audience for music in general has grown globally. Commercialism has taken advantage of this continuing increase in consumption by mass-producing musical types appealing to millions around the world. The large part of the global population in Africa and Asia continues to be an excellent market for Western goods, including music. It is interesting to learn that the total sales of sound recordings have tripled during the past decade. Popular and urban music have sold the most. Although some African nations, such as Egypt, Senegal, and Nigeria, have established their own companies, the top six record-producing countries are, according to the quantity imported, the United States, Japan, the USSR, the United Kingdom, the German Federal Republic, and France.[2]

Public libraries in most African cities are operated by foreign cultural offices and embassies, such as American, British, French, and German information centers. These libraries often make sound recordings and films available for listening and viewing. The information obtained is often prejudicial to the interests of Africans; rarely, if at all, are there materials that advance education about black cultures.

The following two chapters discuss Euro-American elements in African music and how they brought about a new style "third-stream" music.

[2]*Ibid.*

Bibliography

MENON, NARAYANA, "The Influence of the Mass Media on Tomorrow's Public." Unpublished paper read at the World Music Week Conference, Montreal, 1975.

14 Euro-American Elements in African Music

Music change is a phenomenon that is taking place all over the world. It is frequently brought about by changes in the social, political, and administrative conditions of a country. We can approach the study of music change in Africa under three, often interrelated, headings: *musical adoption, acculturation*, and *innovation*.

Musical adoption deals with the substitution of alien forms of music in place of the native ones. The reasons are complex, and they cannot be discussed fully here. Generally speaking, it has taken place in Africa as the result of close cultural contact with the West. With very few exceptions, almost the entire continent of Africa has undergone long periods of European colonization. Hence, the legacy of European domination in Africa has prompted the absorption and adoption of European cultural traits. Those

Africans who underwent the bitter experience of slavery were made to feel inferior to Europeans. Africans have been made to believe and conceive that their own native arts are inferior to those that are European. This negative psychological state has made most Africans blindly adopt European ways.

For example, the Nigerian composer *Fela Sowande* (born 1905) described how strong the European influences were in his own youth in the following statements:

> At the time, we were all busy trying to get ourselves brainwashed. Nothing that was Yoruba was good. Somehow, anything traditional was linked to paganism, heathenism, and it couldn't possibly have any good thing about it. You know, we were all brainwashed, and I was, too.[1]

[1]Eileen Southern, "Conversations with Fela Sowande, High Priest of Music," p. 92.

112

The Europeanized African composer living in this milieu faces a grave dilemma. His profession requires symphony orchestras, trained vocalists, concert halls, and, most of all, appreciative audiences for his work—all totally lacking in most African nations.

When traditional forms of music no longer satisfy the artistic needs of a society, they are either completely abandoned, in which case they disappear, or are partially modified through the processes of *innovation* and *acculturation*.

Remarkable changes in music are observed in the large cosmopolitan cities of Africa. The new styles of music that blend African and European elements are often referred to as *neo-folk, acculturated,* or *urban music.* The European elements include performance of music on stage, the construction and use of theaters for music and dramatic presentations, a fee-paying audience to attend performances, salaried performers, and establishment of dance groups and marching bands.

Urban Dance Music

Urban society is not bound by the laws of ethnic culture. And *urban music* is an expression of this society. It is performed live in most cities. The performers of urban music blend characteristics derived from European-American sources with those that are traditionally African. Today the strongest influence comes from American jazz, Caribbean calypso rhythms, and other types of music such as rock 'n' roll. Disco dancing and music are fast gaining popularity in many cities.

Problems arise, however, when we attempt to classify urban music in Africa into types and kinds. American-style *dance bands* perform acculturated dance music on exclusively European instruments. These bands constitute the most common type of urban music. The African performers are formally trained in European music theory, staff notation, and rudimentary harmony. They employ alien, primarily black American techniques as vehicles when performing musical items from African traditional sources. In other words, the leaders of the bands write compositions and arrangements based on African folk music. These jazzed-up arrangements use simple harmonic accompaniments, which often are restricted to the tonic, subdominant, and dominant chords. Other external influences on urban music also come from Latin America, the Middle East, and Asia as well as from the urban music of other neighboring African countries.

In addition to urban bands that use European instruments exclusively and read music from scores written in European staff notation, there are bands that play improvised or memorized music only on authentic or modified African instruments. This kind of band does not use notation of any kind.

Ethiopia, for example, has two kinds of urban bands—*yebahil orchestra* ("folklore orchestra") and *zemenawi or-*

chestra ("modern orchestra"). The members of the *zemenawi orchestra* serve as an ordinary dance band, employ Western instruments entirely, and play acculturated Ethiopian, African, Latin American, and largely Afro-Americanized musics. The *yebahil orchestra*, comprising traditional musical instruments played by traditionally dressed performers, presents versions of native musical idioms. The very name of their ensemble, "orchestra," is Western; each member musician prefers to be called an "artist" (after Hollywood) instead of the traditional *azmari*—a generic term for musicians derived from the verb *mezemer* ("to sing").

Innovative structural modifications are observed on almost all of the traditional instruments of the *yebahil orchestra*. The *masinKo** (fiddles), contrary* to tradition, are not homemade by the individual performer. Instead they are produced in a factory. They come in three standard sizes: small, medium, and large; this is an element of acculturation along the lines of the string section of a European orchestra. The same approach is applied to the other instruments of Ethiopian traditional music. Electronic amplification devices are even attached to the resonators of chordophones; some, like the *krar*, are also equipped with strings of nylon and wire instead of the traditional gut; they sound like alien instruments, even when performing a native melody. Because of these modifications, the instruments of the *bahil orchestra* produce massive volumes of sound generally preferred by modern city dwellers. Change is apparent in the

area of symbolism in musical instruments. *Bahil* (tradition) often assigned specific roles, extramusical symbolisms, and concepts to musical instruments. The *krar* traditionally possessed the theriomorphic symbolism of a farm ox, the *masinKo* that of a horse. These and many other similar symbolic attributes of music and musical instruments are ignored and forgotten by today's young performers of urban music.

This is a very common trend in other African and Asian countries. Gerhard Kubik has observed a similar phenomenon for many years in Kampala (Uganda):

> The *Heart Beat of Africa*, Uganda's National Orchestra, is the counterpart of the *yebahil orchestra* in Addis, one could say. It comprises traditional musical instruments from all over Uganda, mixing up traditions of the most different ethnic groups—and, of course, the musicians claim authenticity for their daily rehearsed pieces.[2]

Nketia has also observed the presence of change in Ghana and the emergence of new musical traditions as a result of the forces of acculturation.[3]

Highlife is one of the oldest types of urban music of sub-Saharan Africa performed in the dance halls and nightclubs. According to Atta Mensha, its origin dates back to the marching bands formed by disbanded Ghanaian and West Indian soldiers before the turn of the century.[4] It certainly became most popular toward the end of the 1960s, when

---

*The glottalized consonant sounds of the Amharic language—*K* and *C*—are indicated by capital letters; they do not have English equivalents. To sound *K*, the tongue is formed as in *k* but exploded.

[2]Ashenafi Kebede, "Modern Trends in Traditional Secular Music of Ethiopia," *The Black Perspective in Music*, 4, no. 3 (Fall 1976), 289–301.

[3]J.H.K. Nketia, "Modern Trends in Ghana Music," pp. 330–335.

[4]Atta Annan Mensah, "Music South of the Sahara," p. 187.

most hotels and nightclubs employed resident bands to meet the musical needs of their dancing patrons. American popular music, jazz, and calypso have had a marked influence on highlife. Jazz instruments—saxophones, trumpets, vibes, string bass, guitars—are often combined with a variety of African idiophones and membranophones, such as drums, rattles, bells, and so on. The sizes of the bands vary from small combos of four to large orchestras of fourteen performers. Songs are often sung accompanied by spirited dance rhythms. The themes and texts of these songs are often borrowed from West African traditional songs.[5]

A dance form known as *l'arab* or *tarab* is popular in the Afro-Semitic and Islamized regions, which includes the entire North and Northeast as well as the Muslim areas of West and East Africa. It is characterized by the long melismas and highly ornamented melodies of the vocalist accompanied by oriental instruments such as the *'ud, rbab,* and *tabl* mixed with European violins, guitars, and pianos. Unrequited love is the theme of most songs. It is a style of music popular today in many major African cities such as Cairo, Khartoum, Dar es Salaam, Tunis, Casablanca, and Mogadishu. (Very similar styles, both in musical text content and performance practice, are commonly heard in the cities of the Near and Middle Eastern countries, including the Arab section of Jerusalem, Beirut, and Teheran.[6])

Other names of popular dance music of the 1960s and '70s include *Congolese rhumba*, which originated in the republics of Zaire and Congo. As its name implies, it is strongly influenced by Afro-Cuban and Latin American rhythms. *Kwela*, another powerful dance form among youth, originated in South Africa (Johannesburg) and spread wildly throughout Central and South Africa. *Kwela* incorporated jazz idioms with African popular musical practices.[7]

Basic Terms

If you aren't sure what each of the following terms means, look back at the text, where they appear in italic type. Additional information about some of them may also be found by checking the index.

musical adoption	masinKo	neo-folk music	bahil orchestra
innovation	krar	acculturated music	highlife
		urban music	l'arab
		dance bands	tarab
		yebahil orchestra	Congolese rhumba
		zemenawi orchestra	Kwela
		azmari	

[5]Listen to side one, band 3 of *Voices of Africa: High-Life and Other Popular Music.*

[6]The author has traveled and undertaken fieldwork in these areas.

[7]Read also John Blacking, "Trends in the Black Music of South Africa, 1959–1969," pp. 195–215.

Bibliography

BLACKING, JOHN, "Trends in the Black Music of South Africa, 1959–1969," *Musics of Many Cultures*, ed. Elizabeth May. Berkeley, California: University of California Press, 1980, pp. 195–215.

KEBEDE, ASHENAFI, "Modern Trends in Traditional Secular Music of Ethiopia," *The Black Perspective in Music* 1(3—1976):289–301. "Musical Innovation and Acculturation in Ethiopian Culture," *African Urban Studies* 6(1980):77–88.

MENSAH, ATTA ANNAN, "Music South of the Sahara," *Musics of Many Cultures, op. cit.,* pp. 172–194.

NKETIA, J.H. KWABENA, "Modern Trends in Ghana Music," *Readings in Ethnomusicology.*

New York: Johnson Reprint Company, 1971, pp. 330–335.

SOUTHERN, EILEEN, "Conversations with Fela Sowande, High Priest of Music," *The Black Perspective in Music* 4(1—1976):90–104.

Discography

Something New from Africa. Decca LK 4292.

Stars of West Africa: High Life Hits. Vols. 1 & 2. Decca WAL 1023.

Voices of Africa: High-Life and Other Popular Music by Saka Acquaye and His African Ensemble. Edited by Kenneth S. Goldstein and Saka Acquaye. Nonesuch H-72026.

The World of Miriam Makeba. RCA Victor LPM 2750.

15 Third-stream African Music

For the past decade, research in the area of music change has been an important branch of *ethnomusicology*, a young discipline that is often described as an objective study of music in culture. However, the field has not kept pace with the overwhelming changes in music that are taking place in this fast-moving world of mass communication. Aside from the modern urban dance music styles discussed in the last chapter, the emergence of extended forms of third-stream music is apparent in the works of today's African composers. The works of these contemporary African composers still remain beyond the scope of ethnomusicology and musicology. African composers of the third-stream type living in this milieu feel abandoned and ignored by both the artistic and the scholarly communities of Europe and America as well as by the people of their native lands. To make matters still worse, concert halls, electronic studios, symphony orchestras, trained performers, and, most of all, appreciative audiences of serious experimental and new works are almost totally lacking. Hence, most of Africa's composers of third-stream music have taken residencies in Europe and the United States. (This also applies to most well-known Africans in the visual and performing arts.)

The oldest African composer, the Nigerian *Fela Sowande* (born 1905) writes exclusively for European instruments according to Western choral and symphonic traditions. Southern tells us that he "was a boy soprano in the Episcopal Church in Lagos, Nigeria, and studied music as a child with T.K.E. Phillips, the church's organist and church master."[1] He obtained his bachelor of music degree from the University of London. Sowande's remarkable career has earned him international recognition and nu-

[1]Eileen Southern, "Conversations with Fela Sowande, High Priest of Music," p. 91.

merous honors and awards: in 1956 Queen Elizabeth II bestowed upon him the MBE (Member of the British Empire) for "distinguished services in the cause of music"; in 1972 he earned an honorary doctorate of music from the University of Ife, Nigeria.

Fela Sowande lived in London and worked as a jazz musician in the 1930s; he introduced a series of programs in African music for the BBC in the 1940s. His career as a composer-conductor reached its high point when the BBC Symphony Orchestra premiered his work *Africana* in 1944. Sponsored by the State Department, he came to the United States in 1957 to give organ concerts. He later became a permanent U.S. resident and has taught in many universities as professor of African and Afro-American music. He has also conducted many major orchestras, including the New York Philharmonic. Sowande's best known compositions include *Africana, A Folk Symphony,* and *African Suite.*

Akin Euba is another Nigerian composer who holds the diplomas of Fellow of the Trinity College (London) in pianoforte performance and composition. He studied with Nketia and obtained his Ph.D. from the University of Ghana at Legon. Since 1963 Euba has devoted himself to the study of African traditional music, particularly the music of the Yoruba, and has produced compositions making use of elements derived from his ethnic heritage. These compositions include *Chaka* (1970), a setting of a dramatic poem by Leopold Sedar Senghor; *Dirges* (1972), for speakers, singers, instrumentalists, and dancers (using poems by African authors); and *Two Tortoise Folk Tales in Yoruba* (1975), a musical drama for Nigerian instruments

using texts by Adeboye Babalola. Professor Euba also composed the *Festac 77 Anthem* for the Second World Black and African Festival of Arts and Culture held in Lagos, Nigeria. This particular anthem is written for four-part choir and jazz combo including piano, drum set, congo drums, and string bass. The instrumental parts utilize improvisation in an American swing style. The English text of the anthem excluding the refrain, is excerpted from a well-known poem by Afro-American Margaret Walker titled *For My People.** Professor Euba is currently serving as director of the Center for Cultural Studies at the University of Lagos, Nigeria.

Other Nigerian composers of third-stream music include Akinola Akinyele, Samuel Akpabot, Ayo Bankole, Wilberforce Echezona, Lazarus Ekwueme, Adam Fiberissima, Felix Nwuba, Alphonso Okosa, T.K.E. Phillips, and Joshua Uzoigwe.

Many African composers write extended music utilizing the materials of their native tradition through the process of innovation. Priority is given to the propagation and advancement of one's heritage rather than to musical originality. The Ghanaian *Ephraim Amu* is a good example of an African composer whose contributions exhibit a close relationship with the stylistic characteristics of Ghanaian traditional music. His long career goes back to the 1920s, when, as a teacher, he recreated contemporary music using traditional themes in order to meet the new lifestyles of his students.

*Afro-American Margaret Walker was born in Birmingham, Alabama. Her poem *For My People* has become a source of inspiration for black people in their continued struggle against oppression and racism in the USA.

"Besides paving the way for a new type of music," Nketia writes, "he has also helped in establishing a tradition of written African music in Ghana."[2]

J.H. Kwabena Nketia is recognized in Ghana primarily as a composer who interprets the material of his native tradition into contemporary idioms. (He is also admired as a brilliant administrator.) Titles of his compositions include *Builsa Work Song for Piano, Bolga Sonata for Violin and Piano,* and *Canzona for Flute, Oboe, and Piano.* Author of the textbook *The Music of Africa* and numerous scholarly articles, he is internationally known as a prominent specialist of the music of sub-Saharan Africa and one of the most outstanding ethnomusicologists in the world. Professor Nketia serves currently as director of the Institute of African Studies at the University of Ghana in Legon. In addition, he has served as head of the program of ethnomusicology at the University of California in Los Angeles, where he has been on the faculty of the department of music for more than ten years.

N.Z. Nayo, Atta Annan Mensah— also a well-known ethnomusicologist— and Ato Turkson are a few of several contemporary composers in Ghana.

Francis Bebey, former head of UNESCO's music division, is best known as a guitar soloist. This talented Cameroonian is also a composer, poet, author, and administrator. He is well known in the West for his book *African Music: A People's Art,* which is widely read in Europe and America. His musical settings of other people's poems have brought him fame as a performer and composer. His solo pieces include *Tingrela,* a work dedi-

[2]J.H.K. Nketia, "Modern Trends in Ghana Music," p. 334.

cated to a village in Upper Volta; *Song of Ibadan;* and *Concerto for an Old Mask.* His familiarity with and knowledge of African urban music—especially *ashiko,* highlife of the Cameroon, Pygmy vocal techniques, jazz guitar (of Segovia), and Cuban *guajiro*—are demonstrated in his settings of *The Meaning of Africa* and *Breaths,* poems by Sierra Leone's Abioseh Nikol and Senegal's Birgo Diop, respectively. Bebey's impressive techniques include use of the yodel when he sings (in *Breaths,* for instance) and production of percussive sound effects on the resonator and strings of his guitar.

There is no doubt that the growth of Western-style African institutions and organizations have been detrimental to African tradition as a whole. The establishment and popularity of Western-style governments, with their defense, educational, and propaganda systems, throughout Africa has accelerated the emergence and popularity of military and school bands as well as college and university choruses.

Through foreign economic aid obtained by African cultural departments, musical instruments for military and school bands are often bought abroad at exhorbitant prices. Foreign band conductors are hired at the highest salary levels. Some of these foreign personnel become naturalized African citizens. In most cases, university choruses were started by European bandleaders or their African students. European missionary schools in particular had a marked influence on sub-Saharan African Christian musical practices and singing of hymns in four-part arrangements.

In Ethiopia, for example, the Armenian *Kevork Nalbandian* started the European-style band tradition in the early

1940s. He also composed the most popular national anthem sung during Haile Selassie's reign (1930–1974). His cousin, *Nerses Nalbandian*, a naturalized citizen of Ethiopia, advanced a four-part choral tradition in Addis Abeba* that blended elements from Armenian and Ethiopian urban music. Because of his use of four-part harmony laced with a heavily urbanized boogie-woogie rhythmic background, as opposed to the monophonic-textured nonrhythmic styles of most of Ethiopia's traditional music, Nerses Nalbandian's compositions can be categorized and studied under *musical adoption*. It is interesting to note here that Nerses systematically incorporates in his compositions ornamental and decorative sound effects borrowed directly from Amhara and Armenian folk music. Most of his song texts, however, are written and sung in Amharic on serious traditional themes that deal humorously with social reform and unrequited love. For example, the text of his *anchi bale-Tela* is about barley and the traditional women who make barley mead, called *Tela*, as a livelihood. *Tela*, a native beer, is portrayed in the song as an addictively poisonous beverage that has gradually driven men from mild intoxication to drunkenness and finally to insanity. He describes the barley makers as greedy and ignorant women who rob their clients out of both their money and their life. Nalbandian's choral works are undoubtedly intended to be both musically and morally educational to high school and college youths, who often sing and listen to them.

Ethnomusicologists often crossed

*Although commonly spelled Addis Ababa, the spelling version that appears in this book is based on the correct Amharic pronunciation.

over into the field of composition or performance while undertaking comparative analysis of musical systems of two seemingly diverse cultures far apart in geographical location. This particularly applies in my case, I have found close cultural proximity between Japanese *sokyoku* and Amhara *azmari* music in the systems of tuning, performance, use of ornamental subtleties, and general aesthetic principles. My compositions *Koturasia* (for clarinet, Japanese *koto*, and violin) and *Soliloquy* and *Mot* (both for voices, Japanese *koto*, and flute) have been performed at Japan Auditorium in New York City and several universities including Brandeis, Florida State, and Queens College.

A few soloist-composers, like Sudanese *'ud* player *Hamza El-Din*, build their entire compositions solely on elaborate Islamic-Sudanic melodic themes. In breathtaking performances, Hamza interprets a Nubian chant, *The Water Wheel*, with hypnotic effect; through the tonal repetitions of the *'ud* he communicates the timeless cycles of pastoral life embodying all the wonder in the infinity of ripples around the majesty of the Nile. His performances in the United States have received highly positive reviews from papers such as *The New York Times*, *The Woodstock News*, and *The New Age*.

Another remarkable contemporary composer from the oriental African zone is the Egyptian-born *Halim El-Dabh*, who has published over fifty musical scores. His *Concerto for Durbakka* was premiered in 1959 by the American Symphony Orchestra, conducted by Leopold Stokowski. He invented a new system of notation for writing the part of the *durbakka*, a vase-shaped Egyptian drum of clay and fishskin (that is traditionally symbolic of earth and water). El-Dabh's musical vocabulary is rooted in his Afro-Arabic heritage. His compositions are devoid of Western harmonic progression; instead, one experiences heterophonic and polyphonic elements very characteristic of the music of the Nile Valley cultures, elements that have been reintroduced to Western music by Stravinsky and others. Again following his Egyptian heritage and background, many of El-Dabh's compositions integrate and correlate dance, folklore, poetry, and singing with new meanings in space and sound. His *Clytemnestra*, which premiered in New York with choreography by Martha Graham, is a dance opera which has been hailed as a milestone in American theater. This success led to his symphonic music for the ballet *Lucifer*, performed by Rudolf Nureyev and Margot Fonteyn and choreographed by Martha Graham, which premiered in 1975. Halim El-Dabh is currently serving as professor of music at Kent State University.[3]

Preservation and Presentation of African Music

Since the early 1960s, a remarkable upsurge of national consciousness has been sweeping the continent of Africa. The Organization of African Unity (OAU) was founded in 1963, with headquarters in Addis Abeba. Over the past fifteen years, annual festivals, such as the World Festival of Black and African Arts and Culture, have demonstrated the increasing importance African governments are giving to the presentation and advancement of black culture, both traditional and contemporary. Other international festivals, such as the Shiraz-Persepolis Festival, held every year since 1967 in Iran, and the international congresses and meetings of the International Music Council (IMC) and the International Institute for Comparative Music Studies and Documentation (IICMSD), have presented the representative artists of African and Asian traditional music to worldwide audiences in live as well as recorded performances.

In this late-twentieth-century day of mass media, worldwide air transportation, and telecommunication, most musicians anywhere and of whatever racial origin are often involved in the study of world music. Some schools in the United States have even made the study of non-European music a requirement for graduating with a music degree.* Topics such as preservation and presentation of traditional music, music education in the countries of Africa and Asia, African elements in Afro-American music, improvisation, and musical notation, are themes of great academic interest to national and international organizations, societies, committees, institutes, and universities around the world. In this age of worldwide cultural diffusion, the problem of maintaining ethnic values

[3]Halim El-Dabh previously served as music director in the Creative Arts Center of the University at Addis Abeba.
*At Florida State University, for example, a course in world music is required of all undergraduate music majors working toward a degree.

and traditional characteristics remains a complex area without solution.

Although the number of Africans, Asians, and Afro-Americans in the Society of Ethnomusicology is growing, and their contributions increasing, the society is still dominated by Caucasian scholars. With a few outstanding exceptions, European and American ethnomusicologists and educators still approach the study of African music with the erroneous but common assumption that all non-European traditions form an inferior stage of development to that of European music. Outstanding representatives of Asian and African countries have repeatedly established that European conceptions, interpretations, and reactions to music are quite different from those in non-European cultures.[4]

Serious doubts continue to be raised concerning the applicability of European staff notation to transcribe the music of Africa and Asia. Music in African and Afro-American traditions depends largely on improvisation, re-creation, and variation rather than duplication and reproduction of sound from the printed page. African traditional music transcribed in European staff notation "misleads Western musicians who, in their characteristic ethnocentric manner, tend to interpret any music in their own terms, without reference to the tradition it is intended to represent."[5]

Western musicians often experience difficulty in understanding or defining *improvisation*, the art of spontaneous composition highly developed in the performance of music in many non-European cultures. Mastery of a musical language, knowledge of one's own culture, highly developed technique, artistry, creative imagination, discipline, and an ability to convey, re-create, develop, elaborate, and communicate meaningfully ideas through performance make musical improvisation possible. Improvisation is free, while notation is fixed. European notation is suited for most forms of European music; however, it is inadequate for writing the works of certain European contemporary composers. It should not be applied to non-European music. According to French-born *Alain Daniélou*—a leader of a movement against ethnomusicology in the 1960s, spokesman of the International Music Council (UNESCO), and director of the International Institute for Comparative Music Studies and Documentation (IICMSD)—European staff notation alters profoundly the essence and evolution when it is applied to music in African and Asian cultures.[6] He further advises Asians and Africans to honor and promote the values of their musical heritage instead of blindly following the footpaths of Occidental or Euro-American artists and scholars.[7] Daniélou con-

---

[4]Read Evertt Helm's "Report: IMC Congress," p. 45.
[5]This is a quote taken from Nketia's unpublished report "The Musical Languages of Sub-Saharan Africa." The report was presented at the Meeting on Musical Traditions in Africa organized by UNESCO and held in Yaounde, Cameroon, February 23–27,

1970. Also see Ashenafi Kebede's *The Music of Ethiopia*, p. 194, and Bruno Nettl's *Theory and Method in Ethnomusicology*, pp. 120–128.
[6]Personal communications. See also Daniélou's "Musical Education in Africa and Asia," pp. 17–25.
[7]Personal communications. See also Arthur Tomson's "Report: Conference on Music Education in the Orient," pp. 46–50.

siders the contemporary styles of African music—such as the urban music styles, arrangements of traditional music, and the other forms discussed in this chapter—to be inferior forms of Euro-American music.

Current ethnomusicological concepts advanced by David McAllester, Alan P. Merriam, Mantle Hood, Kwabena Nketia, and others have awakened many Euro-American students of ethnomusicology to the need to revise and question many remarks made by earlier writers concerning the study of music in African and Afro-American cultures. The growing population of black and Asian ethnomusicologists has definitely produced positive changes in methodology as well as in attitude. The scope of ethnomusicology has become so broad that it is impossible to know the whole field. The approaches applied to the study of music in culture are varied and numerous. With technological advancement, such as audio-visual recording of artists and use of the computer to analyze sound materials, I would not be surprised if staff notation becomes a thing of the past in the very near future.

There is no doubt that technology has turned the world into a global village. Change is inevitable. Even Western traditions often taken for granted are being impregnated daily by elements largely coming from Africa and Asia. African and Afro-American speech mannerisms, handshakes, hairdos, dance movements, and performance practices of music are imitated by youths all over the world. When critics write about Western influences, they are often talking about the dissemination of musical elements coming from black and popular American musical styles. Jazz is also influenced by Indian classical music. On the other hand, the diversity and charm of world cultures is threatened as European technology standardizes everything in our lives from music and dress to transportation and food. The well-known Vietnamese musicologist Tran Van Khe says that we are all being sucked into the mainstream of standardization where life loses all charm, unless some thought is given to the preservation of the great musical traditions that belong to all mankind.[8]

Dr. McAllester, on the other hand, maintains a different view. He puts it eloquently as follows:

> After all our impulses to cherish and protect, we should realize that human culture is not a flower with fragile petals ready to drop at the first frosty touch of a new idea. Culture is more like an irresistible plague, pandemic to humankind. New ideas are the food it feeds on, and these can no more be stopped than the perpetuation of life itself. The musical manifestations of culture are, by their sonorous nature, highly evident. They give public notice of the spread of culture.[9]

Hopefully, the complex topic of musical change will inspire an enlightening discussion among all of the readers of this book.

[8]Tran Van Khe, "Present and Future Preservation and Presentation of Music and Dance," paper read at the World Music Week Conference held in Montreal, Canada, 1975.

[9]David P. McAllester, "The Astonished Ethnomuse," p. 181.

Basic Terms

If you cannot identify the terms, titles, or names that follow, look back at the text, where they appear in italic type. Additional information about some of them may also be found by checking the index.

ethnomusicology
Fela Sowande
Africana
A Folk Symphony
African Suite
Akin Euba
Festac 77 Anthem
For My People
Ephraim Amu
J.H. Kwabena Nketia
Francis Bebey
African Music: A People's Art
ashiko
guajiro

Kevork Nalbandian
Nerses Nalbandian
musical adoption
anchi bale-Tela
sokyoku
azmari
Hamza El-Din
The Water Wheel
Halim El-Dabh
Concerto for Durbakka
durbakka
Clytemnestra
Lucifer
improvisation
Alain Daniélou

Bibliography

DANIÉLOU, ALAIN, "Musical Education in Africa and Asia," *The World of Music* 10(2—1968):17–25.

EUBA, AKIN, *Festac 77 Anthem.* Nigeria: University of Lagos, 1977.

———, "Traditional Elements as the Basis of New African Art Music," *African Urban Notes* 5(4—1970):52–62.

HELM, EVERETT, "Report: IMC Congress," *The World of Music* 10(4—1968):44–47.

KEBEDE, ASHENAFI, *The Music of Ethiopia: Its Development and Cultural Setting.* Ann Arbor, Michigan: University Microfilms International, 1971.

MCALLESTER, DAVID P., "The Astonished Ethno-muse," *Ethnomusicology* 23(2—1979):179–189.

NETTL, BRUNO, *Theory and Method in Ethnomusicology.* London: The Free Press of Glencoe, 1964.

NKETIA, J.H. KWABENA, "Modern Trends in Ghana Music," *Readings in Ethnomusicology.* New York: Johnson Reprint Corp., 1971, pp. 330–335.

SOUTHERN, EILEEN, "Conversations with Fela Sowande, High Priest of Music," *The Black Perspective in Music* 4(1—1976):90–104.

TOMSON, ARTHUR, "Report: Music Education in the Orient," *The World of Music* 10(1—1968):46–50.

Discography

Black Composer Series. Performed by the London Symphony Orchestra. Conducted by Paul Freeman. Includes Fela Sowande's composition *African Suite.* Columbia M–33433.

Concert pour un vieux masque: Pieces pour guitare. Music of Francis Bebey. Cover notes by Marcel Leclerc. French Philips P70–4681L.

Intsholo. Compositions by African Composers. Performed by the Johannesburg African Music Society. Conducted by Ben Xatasi and Michael Rantho. GALP 1350.

Pentatonism & Microtonality. Compositions by Ashenafi Kebede. Performed by the Hungarian State String Orchestra and Fusako Yoshida, Master of Japanese Koto. International Music P.O. Box 20291, Tallahassee, FL 32304.

V
AFRICAN MUSIC IN THE WESTERN HEMISPHERE

16 The Music of Black Americans

At the beginning of the fifteenth century, the Portuguese made contact with West Africa and found a number of well-established kingdoms along the Guinea Coast and at the mouth of the Congo River. Slavery was then in existence, instituted by the African states and kings. The Portuguese later established commercial relations with these kingdoms, and the first items traded to the Western world were slaves. As the trade increased, Europeans began to realize that slaves in Europe would not be profitable because the number of jobless European farmers increased dramatically.

In the meantime, the new settlers in America were beginning to cultivate their land and plant crops. Those American Indians who had been enslaved, forced to work the crops and live on plantations, died in large numbers from maladjustment to the European culture.

The alternative was to try African slaves. Starting from 1517, the slaves imported from West and Central Africa to Europe had proved to be a hardy and adaptable race of people. The first batch of twenty African slaves arrived on the eastern seaboard of the United States in 1619. Eileen Southern, a well-known black historian and author of *The Music of Black Americans*, tells us that they "were to continue to come for more than two hundred years, brought at first in small groups (called 'parcels'), then later by the shipload, clamped in irons and wedged into foul vessels so closely together that there was hardly enough room for movement." The slave sources included Senegal, Guinea, Gambia, Sierra Leone, Liberia, Ivory Coast, Togo, Dahomey (Benin), Nigeria, Cameroon, Gabon, and Western Congo. Members of the Mandingo, Baoulé, Fon, Yoruba, Ibo, Fanti,

127

Fulani, Ashanti, Jolof, and Hausa tribes were among those that were sold as slaves.[1]

Because of their ability to endure and their spiritual strength, Africans were able to survive as slaves among Europeans of both the Old and the New World. Unlike the American Indians, they were not affected by European diseases; in fact, they often remained healthy, even though laboring under the most inhuman conditions. It is during this period of slavery that we witness the birth of a powerful musical expression conceived as the result of the black man's struggle for his survival and freedom.[2]

In his classic book *The Souls of Black Folk*, W.E.B. Du Bois gives a good description of slave songs:

> What are these songs and what do they mean? I know little of music and can say nothing in technical phrase, but I know something of men, and knowing them, I know that these songs are the articulate message of the slave to the world.... They are the music of an unhappy people, of the children of disappointed; they tell of death and suffering and unvoiced longing toward a truer world, of misty wanderings and hidden ways.[3]

The African chiefs and Arab traders who supplied slaves to the world market captured them by any available means; it is true that many of the slaves died from beatings, malnutrition, overcrowding, disease, mass murder, and suicide. Those Africans who were captured and survived to be herded off to America in chains were often adults, with families and traditional ties. Consequently, they held tenaciously to their old African ways even under the bondage of slavery. This *theory of survivalism*, based on facts advanced by anthropological and ethnomusicological studies, accounts for the retention or *survival* of Africanisms in *all* phases of black American culture, including religious and social attitudes, mannerisms, language (syntax, intonation, accent), names, puns, tales and stories, dance, and music. The agile and impressive movements of most black Americans in athletics, ballet, and dance, their verbal virtuosity and use of double meaning and imagery in speech (often misunderstood as evasion), and, of course, an outstanding sense of rhythm are among the most frequently cited examples of Africanisms in black American culture. Until slave importation was legally stopped in 1864, the African heritage in America was reinforced and strengthened by the continuous arrival of newly purchased natives from Africa.

The African influence on black America has been discounted in the United States for four main reasons: (1) The cultural accomplishments of West and Central African nations, whence the black American slaves came, were almost unknown to the majority of white Americans. It is only recently, within the past thirty years, that ethnomusicologists and anthropologists began to do fieldwork and to discover the complex systems—religious, artistic, social, and political—at the core of African cultures;[4] (2) unfavorable impressions of black people are constantly broadcast by the media (television, radio, movies, books, etc.); (3) black Americans have often at-

[1]Eileen Southern, *The Music of Black Americans*, pp. 3–4.

[2]Rudi Blesh, *Shining Trumpets*, pp. 47–48.

[3]W.E.B. Du Bois, *The Souls of Black Folk*, chapter 14.

[4]Harold Courlander, *Negro Folk Music U.S.A.*, pp. 80–82.

tempted to forget their bitter past, along with Africa and everything reminiscent of it; and (4) the present inferior status of most black people in America has definitely contributed to denials of African survivals in American culture. Consequently, the followers of the *theory of nonsurvivalism*, a theory that denies African survivals in black American culture, argue that black Americans absorbed, learned, and borrowed all they knew—their lifestyle—from the master Euro-American culture. Today it is, of course, next to impossible for us to imagine how people believed that African culture had nothing worth remembering! The most popular and appealing music of the United States today is undoubtedly the African-derived music of black Americans.

On the other hand, the European influence on black American culture should not be underestimated. That both European and African elements were acculturated into the making of the so-called American Negro style is assumed in the *theory of compromise.* It reconciles the opposing survivalist and nonsurvivalist theories. Numerous traits from

English, French, Scottish, and Irish music have been used by black musicians. The enormous French influence on black people is easily recognized in the creole culture of Louisiana and the West Indies; here, the hybridization of French and African elements is evident in the language *(Creole)*, music, dance, religion, folklore, and other aspects of the culture. A few African elements were initially banned by slave owners. For example, tribal activities, including war dances, ceremonials, and rituals that helped organize the slaves into groups, were outlawed. We should also remember that European forms of Christian worship forbade dancing; hence, black slaves were discouraged from making body movements during Christian worship. A few of these objectionable African traits were gradually dropped, or replaced by borrowed European elements. African war dances, for example, have ceased to exist in the practices of black Americans. The polytheistic character of West African religion has been generally replaced by European monotheism as black slaves started to accept the religion of their masters in the United States.

Calls and Cries

Slaves working on American plantations were strictly forbidden to talk to each other; they used *calls* for purposes of communication. Calls attempt to convert speech into song. They often consist of a variety of short messages that were sung solo to attract attention, to warn an inattentive friend at a distance of the approaching white overseer, to break a long monotonous silence, and to summon slaves to work, to eat, or to gather. Although many examples of calls have been recorded by ethnomusicologists, their actual use has faded out in the U.S. with the abolition of slavery and the flight of the blacks from rural to urban localities.

There is no doubt, however, that these calls were African in derivation and that they were sung in African dialects in the early part of slave history. In Africa, peasants melodically call at each other to announce an emergency or news considered important to villagers, to fix a time to go to market, to organize a work gang to farm the land of a sick neighbor, and just to convey greetings to a friend. Calls travel long distances, echoing over mountains and hills. Obviously they provide an interesting topic in the study of *music migration:* how calls have traveled from Africa to the Western Hemisphere as evidenced in African-derived communities like Haiti, Cuba, Trinidad, and Jamaica. In the United States, the Negro calls are also known as *hollers* and *whoopin'*.[5]

Unlike calls, which are primarily used to communicate messages, *cries* express a deeply felt emotional experience, such as hunger, loneliness, or lovesickness.[6] They are half-sung and half-yelled. Vocables are often intermixed in the text. The melodies are performed in a free and spontaneous style; they are often ornamented and employ many African vocal devices, such as yodels, echolike falsetto, tonal glides, embellished melismas, and microtonal inflections that are often impossible to indicate in European staff notation.[7]

Work Songs

At first, the music of the black slave in America was almost entirely African in derivation. The desire to sing while working was very characteristic of the slaves; in sub-Saharan Africa, men and women always sang while working. In the United States, the plantation owners and overseers did not object to the slaves' singing as long as they did their work. As time passed, slave bosses and owners began to notice that the slaves worked harder as they sang. They also observed that there was usually a *lead singer* who set the pace for the group. In fact, when slaves were auctioned, singers with the strongest voices brought top prices. As Courlander aptly puts it:

> The singing leader is as essential to the work gang as the singing leader or preacher is in the church. He must have the feel of the work that is being done, an understanding of the men with whom he is working, and the capacity to evoke both music and motor response.[8]

The themes of work songs vary in direct relation to the labor performed by, and the mood of, the slaves. Topics such as working on the railroad, fishing boats, plantations, and farms are abundant. The sounds of the work often accompany the song; for example, the sound of the axe while cutting trees or chopping

[5]*Ibid.*
[6]For a detailed explanation, listen to the record *Afro-American Music.*
[7]*Ibid.*
[8]Courlander, *op. cit.*, p. 90.

wood, the pounding of grain in a mortar, or the sound of chains in prison camps provide rhythmic background to work songs. Injustice, trouble with the law, escape from prison, and prison life are all important themes of work songs. Women, love, and other subjects drawn from the experiences of slaves are also frequently incorporated into work songs.

Long John is one of the most popular and probably the finest of black American work songs. Though it is found in numerous versions, it deals with a legendary character named Long John who escaped from prison, outsmarted and outran his pursuers—the sheriff, a brigade of his deputies with their bloodhounds—and finally obtained his freedom. Double meanings are an integral part of the text. Reference is also made to the Biblical John.[9]

Long John was sung by black American convicts and prisoners throughout the South as they worked together cutting wood in the forest or in prison camps. It is sung responsorially: the chorus repeats each stanza sung by the leader. The sound of axes, as the prisoners chop logs, provides an *ostinato* rhythm, a regularly recurring beat, in the background. Obviously, the melodic and rhythmic characteristics of the song, the vocal style, and the performance mannerisms of the singers are African-derived.[10] Only the language is Afro-American.

Songs of Black American Children

Like all other societies of the world, the black American culture has specialized songs sung by children; most are game and educational songs that playfully prepare children for the adult world. Children's songs are diversified according to age, sex, or both; there are types sung only by girls, others reserved for boys; some songs are sung by both boys and girls.

Black American children's songs retain numerous elements from their African heritage. European elements that are based on the black experience in America are also present; words, games, and melodic types of European origin have often appeared. But the general approach to performance—the manner or way the songs are sung, the way the games are played, the vocal quality, the postures—draws heavily on African roots. Singing antiphonally and responsorially, handclapping with off-beat syncopation, and body motion are commonly found in children's play songs of both sub-Saharan African and black American traditions.[11]

[9]For a detailed explanation and sound examples, listen to *Afro-American Spirituals, Work Songs, and Ballads.*

[10]*Ibid.* Also see Courlander, p. 90.

[11]Courlander, p. 148.

Ballads

A *ballad* is a narrative song in which the melody is repeated for each stanza. The text, often long, tells a story or a tale, fictional or true, about one or two (usually heroic) characters. Many early black American ballads contain a *refrain*, a repeated musical line often sung by a chorus when it is performed in the African-styled response. However, ballads are often sung solo.

John Henry is probably the most important ballad in the United States. It is a ballad about work. Its origin dates back to 1870. Its theme deals with the construction of the Big Bend Tunnel in the mountains of West Virginia. Modern construction machinery was not standard in those days. Consequently, the face of the rock was hand-drilled by men known as "steeldrivers." Long steel drills were hammered deep into the rock to form holes where explosives were inserted. Parts of the mountain were then blasted away to form a tunnel for railroads to pass through.[12]

According to legend, John Henry, the mightiest of the steeldrivers, was strong enough to work faster than the newly invented steam drill. But alas! Man could not keep up against the machine; John Henry's heart gave out, and he died.

The ballad generally follows the form of strophic songs. One text is molded to the structure of a five-stanza poem. There are also versions with ten and even twenty-two stanzas. Each of the poem's stanzas is set to the same music. This makes the ballad easy to remember.

Faced with hostility, poverty, hatred, prejudice, and often physical torture, the Southern slave created folk tales, stories, and ballads with well-nigh indestructible heroes. The themes of *The Grey Goose Ballad*, for example, are endurance and immortality. The heroic goose resists death after being shot, cooked, carved, and sawed. It was last seen flying over the ocean and victoriously honking "quink-quank" with a gaggle of goslings.[13]

The ballad is often sung without instruments. The repetitive refrain "Lawd, Lawd, Lawd!" is sung by the chorus. The part of the leader has changing text lines, but the melodies are generally the same; thus the story is developed through progressive exposition in the verse. Slaves, especially prisoners, of the Southern states are known to have used this ballad both as a morale booster and as a work song.

Religious Music

The music of black Americans in the United States is not homogeneous. Musical performances in the Northern states are different from those in the South. The black Americans in Louisiana had a different type of music from those in

---

[12]Harold Courlander gives three transcribed versions of "John Henry" in *Negro Folk Music U.S.A.*, pp. 280–286.

[13]For details, listen to *Afro-American Spirituals, Work Songs, and Ballads.*

Georgia. Due to diversity of social values and lifestyles, the music of the educated differs from that of uneducated blacks. This diversity applies to all forms and styles of Afro-American music. In the area of religious music, there are anthems, spirituals, psalmodies, hymns, and, now, gospel songs.

Spirituals hybridize or blend melodies borrowed from early European hymns with African-styled performance practices. Spirituals were conceived from the slave experience in the United States; hence, they are distinctly Afro-American. The texts resound black people's spiritual determination not only to endure and overcome racial hatred but also to aspire to Christian justice, salvation, and immortality.

Though the slaves adopted Christianity and abandoned the worship of African gods, numerous Africanisms have nonetheless been retained to this day in Afro-American religious practices. In many cases, the African polytheistic concepts have been altered to fit European Christian monotheism. We know for a fact that in Haitian-French Catholicism, the Trinity, the Mother of God, and the numerous saints continue to be conceived and worshiped in the manner of African gods, goddesses, and other dieties. The social implications of music remain the same in both African and Afro-American cultures. Spirituals were sung both in and out of the church: at births, baptisms, meetings and while cooking, sewing, and celebrating annual holidays and festivals such as New Year and Christmas. Antiphonal and responsorial singing, the use of vocal slides, moans, groans, and shouts accompanied by dance and handclapping, the practice of possession with body jerks, jumps, and convulsions are all important characteristics common to both Afro-American and sub-Saharan African music.

The *ring shout* of the deep South incorporates music and dance. Dancers form two parallel circles by standing one in front of another. They move counterclockwise, shuffling with their feet to the accompaniment of music provided by the rest of the group. The dancers scream, shout, and make violent movements when they become possessed by the spirit. The ring shout, which provides a therapeutic release of repressed emotions as well as satisfies the needs of religious ritual, is undoubtedly a carryover of the circle dance tradition of West Africa.

The meetings of secret societies practiced in West Africa is mirrored in the praise meetings of black Americans. The houses where these meetings took place developed into independent churches. The earliest known black church in America was in Silver Bluff, South Carolina, established in 1773. Soon after, many religious organizations for black people were formed, including the Free African Society, Absalom Jones's African Episcopal Church, and the African Methodist Episcopal Church.[14] The black church, whether Methodist or Baptist, became a place where black people could freely express their feelings. Music played an important role as a vehicle for achieving this deeply felt emotional experience of "gettin' the spirit." Many of the African elements discussed here continued to be injected in their Christian worship.

European influences have affected black religious music more than any other branch of black music because the

[14]Southern, *op. cit.*, p. 84.

earliest black churches initially used ready-made white spirituals and hymns. In 1801, however, *Richard Allen's Hymn Book* became the first hymnal designed exclusively for an all-black congregation.[15] This book was by no means original; it remolded the great number of white religious songs to meet the linguistic, psychological, and cultural needs of the black folk in America. Afro-American sacred music is a highly controversial topic often discussed by the followers of

the nonsurvivalist theory, as their theory denies any retention of Africanisms in black American music. There is, however, no doubt that black Americans have borrowed heavily from European religious music while simultaneously retaining characteristics and performance practices from their African heritage. Hence, the theory of compromise correctly applies here in any discussion of the processes of Afro-American musical acculturation and syncretism.

Basic Terms

If you cannot identify the terms or titles that follow, look back at the text, where they appear in italic type. Additional information about some of them may also be found by checking the index.

theory
  of survivalism
theory
  of nonsurvivalism
theory
  of compromise
calls
music migration
hollers
whoppin'
cries
lead singer

Long John
ostinato
ballad
refrain
John Henry
The Grey Goose Ballad
spirituals
ring shout
Richard Allen's Hymn Book

---

[15]*Ibid.*, pp. 85–86.

Bibliography

BLESH, RUDI, *Shining Trumpets: A History of Jazz*. New York: Da Capo Press, 1958.

COURLANDER, HAROLD, *Negro Folk Music U.S.A.* New York: Columbia University Press, 1963.

DU BOIS, W.E.B., *The Souls of Black Folk*. Chicago: McClurge Co., 1903.

SOUTHERN, EILEEN, *The Music of Black Americans*. New York: W.W. Norton & Co., 1971.

STEARNS, MARSHALL, *The Story of Jazz*. New York: Oxford University Press, 1958.

Discography

Afro-American Music. Recorded by Dr. Willis James. (1970) Asch Records AA 702.

Afro-American Spirituals, Work Songs, and Ballads. Edited by Alan Lomax. The Library of Congress Music Division. AAFS L3.

Negro Folk Music of Africa & America. Edited by H. Courlander. Ethnic Folkways Library FE 4500.

17 Blues

The *blues* genre of songs originated as the result of black people's bitter experiences in the United States: slavery, racial discrimination, denial of human rights, and intolerable economic conditions. Blacks were placed, as they still continue to be, in the devastating emotional position of indignity, frustration, sadness, and anger. As Samuel Charters correctly describes it, "the blues is the song of men and women who have been hurt, who have been disappointed, who feel the confusion and the isolation of love."[1] As it has been an exceptionally powerful expression of the Afro-American lifestyle, many black Americans claim that the blues genre of songs cannot be fully appreciated without the Afro-American experience. We can assign the blues to four categories: *country blues, racial blues, city blues,* and *urban blues.*

Country and Racial Blues

The *country blues* style exists in oral tradition as a form of personal expression of individuals who sang it in the past and who continue to sing it today. In performance, it belongs to the solo tradition of black American music. Hence, this blues type of song has been historically performed by entertainers without any formal training in music. It is a folk idiom, and, as with most other folk musi-

[1]Samuel Charters, *The Poetry of the Blues,* p. 8.

135

cal styles of the world, the inventor or originator of the blues remains anonymous. Work songs, calls, cries, hollers, and spirituals are predecessors of country blues.

The early blues types might have developed in the Southern states sometime in the early part of the nineteenth century because it was a difficult period of transition from slavery to freedom. The Northern states freed all blacks by 1827. Around the middle of the century, ten percent of the population of four million blacks lived in urban communities of the United States. Although slavery was still enforced in the South, many of the men and women who bought or were given their freedom moved to the large cities of Baltimore, Washington, D.C., Charleston, Mobile, and New Orleans. Most of the black city dwellers were employed as servants and laborers. A few of them were also able to make a living in entertainment and other professions. The blues style was disseminated and popularized by some of these street musicians and lonesome entertainers.[2]

The proclamation of January 1, 1863, abolished slavery in those states that seceded from the Union. It was not until 1865 that formal emancipation came to all the states. The black man had to sing the blues to unburden himself of the cruel and harsh realities of his life; the blues definitely served as a therapeutic release. When emancipation at last came, it did not solve the enormous problems of the nineteenth century antebellum Southern slaves. Even today, over one hundred years after the Civil War ended slavery, black people are deprived of a large part of American equal oppor-

tunity; they live in poverty- and crime-infested black ghettos plagued by the injustices of American life. Thus the blues took deep root and developed as an expression of these discontented people.

Racial blues refers to songs whose content and style are based upon racial distinction between whites and blacks. Simply speaking, black singers have developed song types that are specifically designed to be sung only for blacks and other types only for whites; songs sung only for blacks will be inappropriate for white audiences because they consist of antiwhite slants, protests, and even obscenities; in addition, the meaning of the song texts, their verbal codes and symbolic terms, can be comprehended only by in-group black members who have shared similar experiences.[3] In many cases, country and racial blues are sung in *Gullah*, the black American dialect of the English language that consists of about four thousand words derived from West African languages. The early 78 rpm "race records" of the 1920s provide good examples of songs that were specifically designed for, and bought by, an all-black clientele.

Generally speaking, the blues repertoire for blacks and whites differed both in style and language. For example, "Joe Turner" was sung almost exclusively for blacks.

> They tell me Joe Turner been here and gone.
> They tell me Joe Turner been here and gone.
> They tell me Joe Turner been here and gone.[4]

---

[2]The blues are discussed in Rudi Blesh's *Shining Trumpets*, pp. 98–148.

[3]William R. Ferris Jr., "Racial Repertoires Among Blues Performers," pp. 439–449.

[4]Harold Courlander, *Negro Folk Music U.S.A.*, p. 136.

Sometimes a single line of text, stated three times, suggests a long anecdote quite well understood by black audiences. The legend suggested is about a kindly white man who provided black people with provisions whenever they were in need, when there were droughts, or floods, or when the crops failed. "Around 1892," according to Courlander, "there was a bad flood and people lost everything they had. When the flood receded and they came back to their houses, they found food waiting for them, wood for fuel, and even axes to cut the wood. Joe Turner had been there. Their benefactor's identity was discovered when a general storekeeper some miles away died, and the kindness came to an end."[5] Obviously, only the in-group black participants can understand the meaning of this simple and repetitive blues.

Here is another example of racial blues that is clearly intended for black audiences only:

> The nigger and the white man playing seven up.
> The nigger beat the white man, scared to pick it up.
> He had to bottle up and go.
> Well, your high-power woman shore got to bottle 'em up and go.[6]

The following racial blues is a social commentary. It reflects the injustice and the insult inflicted on the black man.

> Down South when you do anything that's wrong,
> Down South when you do anything that's wrong,
> Down South when you do anything that's wrong,

They'll sure put you down on the country farm.
Put you down under a man called Captain Jack.
Put you under a man called Captain Jack.
Put you under a man called Captain Jack.
He'll sure write his name up and down your back.
Put you down in a ditch with a great big spade.
Put you down in a ditch with a great big spade.
Put you down in a ditch with a great big spade.
Wish to God you hadn't even been made.[7]

Since most whites were very sensitive to disapproving remarks made by blacks concerning their unfair treatment, blues performers removed the black slang, verbal codes, and obscene remarks when they performed before whites. As the result of this racial distinction, the black American singer developed dual-personality traits as a "survival mechanism." One personality is often candid and honest for himself and his race, while the other is superficial and stereotyped for whites.[8]

Blues texts express the emotional concerns of the black man. Unrequited love, sex, loneliness, homelessness, life in prison, poverty, broken homes, and the insecurity of being black in a white society constitute the major themes of the blues. A few of the songs include protest and social commentary. Even the titles of the songs—"Empty Bed Blues," "Prison Blues," "Bedbug Blues," "Whiskey

[5]*Ibid.*
[6]Ferris, *op. cit.*, p. 443.

[7]Samuel Charters, *op. cit.*, pp. 155–156.
[8]Johnson and Odum, *The Negro and His Songs*, pp. 6–7.

Blues," "Overseas Blues"—are short but poignant descriptions of unhappy circumstances. This verbal virtuosity, a carry-over from Africa, is also found in the writings, sermons, puns, riddles, and stories of black Americans. The blues texts deal with strictly secular topics.[9]

Blues texts are constructed in a variety of ways. Songs with a single line that is repeated many times (similar to the example "Joe Turner") probably developed from work songs where the leader-chorus call-response technique required repetition. The early blues used duple or *paired texts* as follows:

> Lay awake and just can't eat a bite.
> She used to be my rider, but she just won't treat me right.[10]

The *three-line stanza*, characteristic of most blues, consists of statement, re-statement, and commentary.

> Woke up this morning, feeling sad and blue,
> Woke up this morning, feeling sad and blue,
> Didn't have nobody to tell my troubles to.[11]

The *four-line stanza* is not uncommon. Sometimes the two-line poetry is broken into four short lines. We start with this:

> I was standing on the corner with my hat in my hand,
> Looking for a woman didn't have no man.

Changes in the text are accompanied by changes in the music. The above two-line verse has been effectively rendered as a four-line text.

> I was standing on the corner,
> I had my hat in my hand.
> I was looking for a woman,
> Woman without a man.[12]

The use of repetitive singles, duples, triples, and quadruple-line stanzas in songs is a common characteristic of vocal music in sub-Saharan Africa. Consequently, the manner in which blues texts are constructed is an Africanism in black American music. We should also mention that West African speech mannerisms, such as tonal glides, accentuations, mouth resonance, and microtonal inflections have survived in black American dialects of English. Consequently, almost the entire genre of Afro-American vocal music consists of unique rhyming schemes, rhythmic structures, vocal dynamics, and syllabic ornaments that have made it irresistibly appealing. The performers often add, drop, or change syllables or words in order to portray the desired feelings and conform to local dialects of English: "de" is used for "the"; "hee" for "here"; "goin" for "going"; "befo' " for "before," rhymed with "go"; and "ain'ta thata good news?" for "ain't that good news?" which stands in turn for "isn't that good news?" Free rhyme or assonance is an important characteristic of blues song texts.

[9]Ashenafi Kebede, "African Music in the Western Hemisphere."

[10]Samuel Charters, *op. cit.*, p. 15.

[11]Eileen Southern, *The Music of Black Americans*, p. 334.

[12]Samuel Charters, *op cit.*, p. 24.

Musical Characteristics of Country Blues

As the country blues exist through the oral method of transmission, they are performed spontaneously in a free solo style. Variation and repetition are the most important characteristics of the melodies. These traditional blues (also known by the misnomer "archaic blues") do not follow rigid melodic patterns that can be cited as a blues formula. A blues song—for example, "Careless Love" — may often be sung in many versions; different soloists perform each blues song in a manner befitting his personal style and preference, depending also on mood, experience, creativity, and the audience. Great diversity thus exists in performance, style, and content. The traditional blues consist of subtle tonal inflections, ornaments, and rhythmic nuances that cannot often be accurately indicated by European notation; country blues cannot be cast into a rigid framework of bars and measures.

For our present purpose, however, suffice it to say again that the melodic structure of most blues is governed by textual considerations. The first line is often repeated with the same melody. Melodic changes often occur with changes in the text. A term of endearment, such as "Oh baby," or vocables such as "oh-ha-ha," an expletive, or an exclamation may sometimes be added or dropped when the first line is repeated. A concluding third line is sung to a second melodic line. Thus we have here statement, restatement, and contrast; the melody parallels the *a a b* arrangement.

Blues melodies generally employ heptatonic scales that are different from the European major-minor diatonic schemes. Many blues songs contain neutral thirds—an interval between the major and minor third—and neutral sevenths—an interval between the European major and minor seventh intervals. These neutral third and seventh intervals are often referred to as blue notes. (They can be produced by sliding on the third and seventh tones of the diatonic major scale.) The fifth and sixth degrees of the blues tonality often correspond to the European major scale, but these tones are occasionally lowered in some blues. As the neutral intervals are found in the musical practices of many African societies, the blues tonality can be explained in terms of the African roots of black American music.

Sophisticated rhythm is a built-in characteristic of almost all blues melodies. It is performed in *isometer*, a term that refers to music without change in meter because of repeated rhythmic patterns. Generally speaking, the isometric organization of rhythm is one of the common factors shared by European and African folk musical styles that have contributed to mutual influences. Most blues adhere to duple meter, with lively off-beat syncopation.

The traditional blues singer often accompanied himself on a musical instrument, such as the guitar or the banjo. Besides the solo instrumental introduction, often played to create mood, and interludes played between verses, the part of the accompanying instruments closely duplicates the vocal melodies. Sometimes, however, tonic, subdominant, and dominant chords are played as accompaniment. This clearly European influence is especially noticeable in city blues and urban blues.

The traditional country blues are genuine expressions of an individual performer moved by deep feelings. Slow movements of the body and facial distortion support the mood of lament. The eyes, mouth formation, head movement, and hand gestures express the text sentimentally and touchingly. The lips and nostrils quiver, enhanced by heartfelt emotional outcries.

Performers of Country Blues

Interest in country blues did not start until the middle of the 1920s. The earliest blues record was made by Papa Charlie Parker in 1924. *Blind Lemon Jefferson* (1897–1930), who accompanied himself on the guitar, recorded his first disc in 1926. Unlike the commercial records produced in studios, many of the country blues, were taped in the field by enthusiastic collectors who considered the natural environment of a blues performer to be an important factor in the quality of his performance. *Huddie "Leadbelly" Ledbetter* (1888–1949) was one of the most important bluesmen who helped advance interest in black American music through his numerous recordings and performances. His style, as recorded by the Folk Song Archives of the Library of Congress, provides excellent examples for the study of country blues. Like Blind Lemon, his model, whom he also once served as a guide, he accompanied himself on the guitar.[13]

Other famous traditional blues performers include *Sounders "Sonny" Terry* (1911–   ), who played on the harmonica instead of the guitar, *Big Bill Broonzy* (1893–1958), and *Blind Boy Fuller* (1903–1940). Terry and Fuller teamed up for a series of recordings and performances.[14]

[13]Eileen Southern, *op cit.*, p. 400.
[14]*Ibid.*

Figure 17.1. Huddie "Leadbelly" Ledbetter. Culver Pictures, Inc.

City Blues

Ever since its invention in 1877, *sound recording* has revolutionized the world of music, East and West. Its application was at first limited to European music. It is believed that the first recordings of non-Western music were the Edison cylinders made by Walter Fewkes of Zuñi and Passamaquoddy Indian songs in 1889.[15] Recordings were then made primarily for academic and archival purposes. Its commercial uses began early in the twentieth century with the establishment and growth of sound producing business enterprises and industries, such as radio stations and recording and publishing companies.

The impact of sound recording on black American music cannot be emphasized enough. After black people found themselves free members of American society, their frame of reference shifted from Africa to America. Without education, skill, or political power, their freedom generally provided a life of unemployment, poverty and frustration. Most moved to urban areas and became part of complex American city life, in such places as saloons, nightclubs, and whorehouses. The white-controlled music business provided material rewards to a few black performers. Spontaneous singing and dancing became rigid rehearsals as these performers tried to record their product in music studios that had prescribed requirements. Using European staff notation, professional musicians arranged the structure of blues according to clearly defined formulas. The African-derived elements in black American music—continuous variation, improvisa-

tion, and other characteristics of oral tradition—were replaced by formalization. Rudi Blesh tells us that due to industrialization and the impact of the communications media, the music of black Americans was packaged like pills for public consumption. In 1920, Okeh Recording Company made the first commercial recording by a black American woman, *Mamie Smith.*[16]

The *city blues*, also known as "classic blues," is thus a standardized version of the country or rural blues. It is often accompanied by a piano or a small ensemble of European instruments. It is interesting to note here that the earliest city blues were recorded with accompaniment provided by African-derived instruments, like the tub, jug, and washboard. *Ma Rainey's* recording of "Traveling Blues," made in 1929, serves us as a good example of this.[17]

The example of city blues in Figure 17.2 adheres to the standardized twelve-bar blues format. The first text line is sung twice; the concluding text is usually different, and it is sung to a varied melodic line. The song is accompanied by the *blues progression* which consists of the tonic, subdominant, and dominant chords. Syncopation is a built-in rhythmic characteristic of most blues. This standardized musical structure of the city blues must be remembered as one of the predecessors of jazz, wherein new improvised or varied melodies are instrumentally performed, accompanied by these chord progressions.[18]

---

[15]See Bruno Nettl's *Theory and Method in Ethnomusicology*, p. 16.

[16]Eileen Southern, p. 397. See also Blesh, *op. cit.*, pp. 146–147.

[17]Frank Tirro, *Jazz: A History*, p. 144.

[18]Stephen Elmer, "The 'American' Art Form," p. 482.

Figure 17.2. City blues.

I woke up dis mornin' an' my head felt bad. I

woke up dis mornin' an' my head felt bad. I was

dreamin' 'bout my baby an' what a time we had.

Urban and Instrumental Blues

The term *urban blues* is applied to the city blues of the 1940s and later. Urban blues are distinguished by big band accompaniment, addition of new instruments—saxophone, electric guitar, etc.—and use of modern amplification devices. The vocal part is important in both ur-

ban and city blues types. The rhyme and melodic schemes often follow the *a a b* format. The basic unit retains either a $\frac{4}{4}$ eight-bar or twelve-bar pattern; these units are at times expanded by doubling them into either a sixteen-bar or twenty-four bar pattern.

Instrumental blues, as the name indicates, is performed without a singer or vocalist. In its early stages, it followed the scheme of the standard vocal blues. Later, however, it gradually developed into a unique and independent instrumental form. Instrumental blues have a formal concept of improvisation that has especially contributed to the development of jazz.[19]

Creators and Performers of Composed Blues

Unlike country blues, which existed in oral tradition, city and urban blues types were scored. The use of European music notation has undoubtedly accelerated the processes in the de-Africanization of black American music.[20] *W.C. Handy* (1873–1958), who ironically called himself "Father of the Blues," wrote the first blues composition, *The Memphis Blues*, in 1909; it was published in 1912. *St. Louis Blues*, (1914) Handy's most famed composition, was performed by *Bessie Smith* in 1925.[21]

Black women played an active role in the American music scene of the 1920s. Ma Rainey (Gertrude Malissa Nix Pridgett), also known as "Mother of the Blues," is recognized as the earliest professional blues vocalist; she made her first recording in 1923. Bessie Smith (1894–1937), the most popular blues singer of the time, was known as "Empress of the Blues." A woman of great talent, her influence on contemporary blues vocalists still remains strong. We have already mentioned Mamie Smith, the lady who made the first commercial record by a black vocalist in 1920. *Crazy Blues*, the title of the song that she recorded, was composed by Afro-American Perry Bradford.[22]

[19]See Frank Tirro, *op. cit.*, p. 145.
[20]Read Alain Daniélou's article "Cultural Genocide."
[21]See Eileen Southern, pp. 337–339.
[22]*Ibid.*, p. 397.

Figure 17.3. Bessie Smith. Culver Pictures, Inc.

Basic Terms

If you cannot identify the terms, titles, or names that follow, look back at the text, where they appear in italic type. Additional information about some of them may also be found by checking the index.

blues
country blues
racial blues
Gullah
paired texts
three-line stanza
four-line stanza
isometer
Blind Lemon
  Jefferson
Huddie "Leadbelly"
  Ledbetter
Sounders "Sonny"
  Terry
Big Bill Broonzy

Blind Boy Fuller
sound recording
Mamie Smith
city blues
Ma Rainey
blues progression
urban blues
instrumental blues
W.C. Handy
The Memphis Blues
St. Louis Blues
Bessie Smith
Crazy Blues

Bibliography

BLESH, RUDI, *Shining Trumpets: A History of Jazz.* New York: Da Capo Press, 1958.

CHARTERS, SAMUEL, *The Poetry of the Blues.* New York: Oak Publications, 1963.

COURLANDER, HAROLD, *Negro Folk Music U.S.A.* New York: Columbia University Press, 1963.

DANIÉLOU, ALAIN, "Cultural Genocide," *The World of Music* 11 (1—1969):28–31.

ELMER, STEPHEN, "The 'American' Art Form," *Music: An Appreciation*, ed. Roger Kamien. New York: McGraw-Hill Book Co., 1976.

FERRIS, WILLIAM R., JR., "Racial Repertoires Among Blues Performers," *Ethnomusicology* 14 (3—1970):439–449.

JOHNSON, GUY B., and HOWARD W. ODUM, *The Negro and His Songs* (2nd ed.). Hatboro, Pennsylvania: Folklore Associated, 1964.

KEBEDE, ASHENAFI, "African Music in the Western Hemisphere," *African Music*. Paris: UNESCO, 1972.

NETTL, BRUNO, *Theory and Method in Ethnomusicology*. London: The Free Press of Glencoe, 1964.

SOUTHERN, EILEEN, *The Music of Black Americans*. New York: W.W. Norton & Co., 1971.

TIRRO, FRANK, *Jazz: A History*. New York: W. W. Norton & Co., 1977.

Discography

Down Home: A Portrait of a People. Folkways Records FA 2691 ABCD.

Jazz: The Blues. Volumes I & II. Frederick Ramsey, Jr. Folkways Records PF 51, PF 53.

Leadbelly. Recorded by John & Alan Lomax. The Library of Congress Recordings EKL-301/302.

Leadbelly Sings Folk Songs. Folkways Records 31006.

Ma Rainey. United Hot Clubs of America 83–85.

Bessie Smith. Columbia 3172-D.

Big Joe Williams. Everest Records FS-218.

18 African-derived Instruments in Black American Music

New Orleans, a city and a seaport near the Gulf of Mexico, was a cultural melting pot par excellence in North America. It accommodated the large multiethnic, multiracial population and provided them with unique cultural opportunities. Because of its geographic location and historical background, it attracted international residents from all over the world. It was a French possession for nearly half a century; thus the French tradition was well established. At first, the large French population was made up of adventurers, priests, thieves, pimps, and women who were recruited in France and sent to New Orleans. The Spanish occupied the city in 1764 and promoted their culture during the thirty-six years of their domination; their population added substantially to the number of residents of European origin. Napoleon Bonaparte got it back for France in 1800 and sold it to the United States after three years. The European population was again increased by the migration of Anglo-Saxons, Italians, and other Euro-Americans from within the United States.[1]

Black people were brought, and encouraged to come, to work on the cotton and sugar plantations, which were the main sources of the city's wealth. The population was made up of people from both West Africa and Haiti, Cuba, and other Caribbean islands. Because of the great cultural tolerance, inherent in the French *laissez-faire* attitude of live and let live, the city constantly attracted new black immigrants. Black people in New Orleans were freely permitted to practice their African-style cultures, including *vodou*, a formalized way of life featuring sorcery and the worship of animistic deities as well as performances of music and dance. Around 1803, half of the 10,000 population of New Orleans was

[1]Rudi Blesh, *Shining Trumpets*, pp. 151–172. See also Marshall Stearns's *The Story of Jazz*, pp. 33–37.

black. The ratio did not change much by the time the population had doubled seven years later in 1810.[2] (It was still forty-five percent in 1970.)

Between 1817 and 1880, African-style instruments were popularly used in the music of black Americans. The instruments were not imported from Africa but made by those slaves who recalled the instruments of their native music before they came to the New World. Especially in New Orleans, where the Negro population was the largest of any American city, most celebrations and rituals were direct survivals of West African traditions. Since some of the black people came from the West Indies (especially Haiti and Cuba), there were also culturally hybrid musical manifestations.[3]

Africanisms were apparent not only in the make of musical instruments but also in the style of performance and types of ceremonials performed in New Orleans's *Congo Square*. It was also known as Place Congo, because some five or six hundred black persons used to meet at the square on Sunday afternoons to perform and dance. They even formed what they considered to be their tribal groups such as Congos, Fon, Dahomey, and Yoruba. Each tribe had its own chief, drum ensemble, and dance group, which competed socially with those of the other ethnic groups. The best ethnic group was acknowledged and rewarded. According to Titcomb, the first New Orleans *Mardi Gras* procession was in 1827. The pageant of decorated floats began in 1857, and it became a yearly activity attended by

almost all the black population of the city. The arrival of Zulu, King of the Africans, who appeared with a huge parade of followers, started the electrifying festivities of the Mardi Gras.[4]

In the early part of slave history, black people were forbidden to play African-style loud drums that might be used for signaling purposes in time of insurrection. Consequently, it is possible that they duplicated a soft-sounding stringed instrument that they had known in Africa, and that was less objectionable to the slave owners and overseers. Among chordophones, the homemade folk banjo was the most popular and has had the longest existence in the New World. The enslaved African singing and strumming on the banjo was known and documented by European writers well before 1700. Thomas Jefferson wrote in 1782 that the instrument proper to the Negroes "is the Banjar, which they brought hither from Africa,..."[5] Banjar, banjor, or *banjo* are derivations from the African *mbanza*. The Senegalese *bania* has been cited as the root of the word. In its early form as a folk instrument, it was made of a half-gourd resonator covered by animal skin, with a wood or bamboo neck and four strings. Unlike the commercial banjo, it is fretless; its strings are made of gut, or horsehair, instead of nylon or metal. The folk banjo is popularly found today in many countries of the Western hemisphere populated by black people, including Martinique, Jamaica, Haiti, Cuba, and the United States.[6]

Another African-style chordophone is the *gutbucket*, also known as the *tub* or washtub. An inverted metal tub acts as a

[2]Personal communications with Caldwell Titcomb. See also Fredrick Kaufman & John P. Guckin's *The African Roots of Jazz*, p. 4.

[3]See Harold Courlander's *Negro Folk Music U.S.A.*, p. 208.

[4]See Blesh, *op. cit.*, p. 154.

[5]*Ibid.*, p. 50.

[6]See Courlander, *op. cit.*, pp. 212–214.

resonator. Sound is produced by slapping a cord attached to the center of the inverted tub against a protruding broomstick. It provides a sort of bass accompaniment.

The instrumental resources of traditional Africa include numerous horns and trumpet types that are made of wood or bamboo. Similar instruments were observed in the musical performances of black Americans at Congo Square. Later on, during the colonial period, they easily adopted and used the European type of brass horns and trumpets. The European harmonica gradually replaced the African-style panpipes. European flutes and clarinets were adopted instead of the various homemade bamboo aerophones of African derivation.

Among idiophones, the *washboard* has been used as a rhythm instrument. The surface may be scraped with a wire, nail, or fingernail. Woodblocks, frying pans, empty foodcans and tins, sticks, and bones all fall under this class of instruments. Idiophones have shown great variety: there have been rattles made of gourds, cans, bottles filled with stones, teeth, and even coins. Sometimes scrapers have been made from jawbones of horses.

African drum types in several sizes and shapes composed the membranophones at an early date. Dances performed included circle dances with predominantly shuffling steps, also characteristic of western Africa, accompanied by a great variety of drums.

It is important to point out here that the music of the slaves was not exclusively African. European-style music and dances also made up an important part of the festivities: there were black persons who performed on European instruments such as trumpets, clarinets, violins, and drums. They also danced to music performed by white dance bands and orchestras. Consequently, the Place Congo was definitely a meeting place of traditions, a melting pot where hybridization took place at a constantly increasing rate. It is the people who participated as children at Congo Square who later formed the first street bands. Many bands started around the 1880s, when the activities of Congo Square began to decline in importance.

During the American Revolution (1775–1783), many black men enlisted and served in the military. Following the Virginia Act of 1776, most of the servicemen from this state were employed "as drummers, fifers, or pioneers."[7] Until 1792, military bands composed of instruments as we know them today did not exist. When it was organized by an act of Congress, black military men were specially assigned to musical tasks. They played on European brass, woodwind, and percussion instruments. This, of course, provides an explanation for the popularity of all-black brass bands after the War of 1812. Most of the members of the bands were accomplished performers with formal training in music during their service in the military. A great number of them read staff notation and used it creatively for purposes of composition. Dance bands were organized that added stringed instruments: the violin, viola, cello, and bass. At the end of their military service, many black Americans made a good living as professional musicians—bandmasters, orchestra leaders, composers, performers, and teachers.[8]

[7]Eileen Southern, *The Music of Black Americans*, pp. 69–77.

[8]Southern, *op. cit.*, p. 77.

Basic Terms

If you aren't sure what each of the following terms means, look back at the text, where they appear in italic type. Additional information about some of them may also be found by checking the index.

vodou

Congo Square

Mardi Gras

banjo

mbanza

bania

gutbucket

tub

washboard

Bibliography

BLESH, RUDI, *Shining Trumpets: A History of Jazz*. New York: Da Capo Press, 1958.

COURLANDER, HAROLD, *Negro Folk Music U.S.A.* New York: Columbia University Press, 1963.

KAUFMAN, FREDRICK, & JOHN P. GUCKIN, *The African Roots of Jazz*. Sherman Oaks, California: Alfred Publishing Co., 1979.

SOUTHERN, EILEEN, *The Music of Black Americans*. New York: W.W. Norton & Co., 1971.

Discography

Folk Music USA. Volume I. Compiled by H. Courlander. Ethnic Folkways Library FE 4530.

Music from the South. Volumes 5 and 10. Frederick Ramsey, Jr. Folkway Records FA 2654 and FA 2659.

The Story of Jazz. Folkway Records FC 7312.

19 Jazz

Historians have designated the 1890s as the high point of black musical achievement in the form of ragtime and *jazz*. However, the origin of the word *jazz* remains a mystery. It is, according to Merriam and Garner, "variously derived from Africa, Arabia, the Creole, French, Old English, Spanish, the Indians, the names of mythical musicians, old vaudeville practices, associations with sex and vulgarity, onomatopoeia, and other sources."[1] There are theories that trace the word to West Africa. Some believe that *jazz* is derived from the Hausa word *jaiza*, a term used to describe the sound of drumbeats.[2] The sound of large buzzing and booming drums is also considered as the onomatopoetic source of the word *jazz*. Some local areas in the South, particularly New Orleans, may have used the word *jass* to refer to the sound of Negro bands sometimes before the turn of this century. However, the term did not become popular in its present spelling and context until around 1915.[3]

Jazz is easier to experience and feel than to define. It is semi-improvised music. The jazz improviser's spontaneous creativity on a theme is highly dependent on his mood and circumstances at the time of a given performance. Consequently, duplication is not possible in most jazz performances of high quality and relative authenticity; neither is it possible to apply European prescriptive notation to jazz. Jazz often uses solo, duet, and simultaneous improvisation by the members of the band. This collective effort to improvise simultaneously as a "chorus" on a theme in a manner that is musically meaningful and artistically gratifying is referred to as the *hot concept* of jazz. The intricate melodic counterpoint and multirhythmic variation em-

1. See Alan P. Merriam & Fradley H. Garner, "Jazz—The Word," pp. 381–382.
2. *Ibid.*
3. *Ibid.*, p. 389.

bodied in this West African hot concept has been obviously transferred to describe a similar development in the heritage of Afro-Americans.[4]

At the beginning, black American music reflected the racial and social revolt of the black people against the white society in the United States. Blues and jazz were considered to be music of the slaves and other ethnic groups at the lowest stratum of American society. In fact, most of the critics of early jazz conceived and described it as vulgar and primitive.[5] Children of white America were warned to keep away from it. Having passed through the processes of acculturation and syncretism, promoted by nonblack commercial exploiters, the media, and recording companies, jazz soon became one of the most appealing and popularly imitated musical expressions of all Americans.

"Buddy" Charles Bolden's (1868–1931) *Ragtime Band*, organized in 1893, is generally considered the first jazz band before the name "jazz" emerged. The music played by this band represented the uniqueness of the black experience in the United States. Although it has assimilated elements from African and European music, it was neither African nor European. Negro bands had previously performed music on the streets. Bolden's band, however, moved closer to European mannerisms and performed on stage—not yet in concert but in dance halls. Bolden was famed for his improvisations on, or *ragging* of, melodic themes on his cornet. Of course, none of the music was then written. The mem-

bers of his band mastered their *riffs*—phrases often repeated behind lead melodies—through the direct learning-by-doing method of instruction.[6] Each performer, however, depended on his own artistic virtuosity when it was time for him to improvise. Performing jazz became a salaried position with the opening of Storyville—a redlight district—in 1897. *Storyville jazz* was thus closely associated with cabarets, bars, whorehouses, sex, and vulgarity. Storyville officially closed in 1917.[7]

From the very beginning of slavery, the black person in America was known as a clown, comic figure, agile dancer, and musician. He was to inspire many artists, composers, and writers around the world. *Stephen Foster* (1826–1864), the well-known composer of *"Old Black Joe,"* *"Old Folks at Home,"* and many other songs, was a good example of one of countless nonblacks who used the black lifestyle as a source of his creations. In blackface minstrelsy, white performers danced and sang on the stage as blacks. It is important also to learn here the ironic fact that it was an all-white band, the *Original Dixieland Jazz Band*, that made the first recording of jazz in 1917. In 1927, Al Jolson, a white actor, starred in the first talking movie, *The Jazz Singer*. The United States of America not only disengaged from its complete dependence on European music but proudly propagated jazz throughout the world as its own unique musical art form.[8]

4. See Ashenafi Kebede's "African Music in the Western Hemisphere," p. 132.
5. See Rudi Blesh's *Shining Trumpets*, pp. 9–10.

6. For the names of the musicians in the band and for detailed information, see Blesh, *op. cit.*, pp. 180–183.
7. Frank Tirro, *Jazz*, pp. 73–75.
8. Frederick Kaufman & John P. Guckin, *The African Roots of Jazz*, pp. 114–123. See also Eileen Southern, *The Music of Black Americans*, pp. 103–104.

Figure 19.1. The Original Dixieland Jazz Band. Brown Brothers.

Classic jazz, the New Orleans–style small-band tradition, moved to other cities (Chicago and New York among others) after the closing of Storyville. The members of the *Hot Five*, a band organized by *Daniel Louis Armstrong* (1900–1971), were the best instrumental soloists of this tradition. The other four were Johnny Dodds (clarinet), Kid Ory (trombone), Lil Hardin (piano), and Johnny St. Cyr (banjo). The greatest cornet, and later trumpet, player of all time, Armstrong was the most important figure in the Jazz Hall of Fame. Author, comedian, and actor, he was also the most recorded of all jazzmen. Although his style later changed with the big bands, Armstrong's early recordings with the Hot Five provided us with the best examples of performance practices of New Orleans or classic jazz with its collective improvisations, remarkable virtuosity of the soloists, rhythmic and melodic counterpoint, and intricate polyphony.

Since the late 1930s black Americans' have shown a growing interest in the so-called Third World cultures—people who are not white. As Malcolm X later said, "He who is not white is colored." Many black Americans converted from Christianity to Islam in the 1940s, and they continue to do so today. African and Arabic names were substituted for

Figure 19.2. Louis Armstrong. Associated Booking Corp., Joseph G. Glass, President.

their European "slave" names. Many jazz musicians also became Muslims and changed their names. For example, the percussionist Kenny Clarke took the name Liaquat Ali Salaam; saxophonish Ed Gregory became Sahib Shihab. Interest in the music cultures of Africa and Asia were particularly notable in the 1960s. *John Coltrane* (1926–1967), regarded as the most important jazz musician of the '60s, was fascinated by *ragas* and *talas*, Indian melodic and metric formulas. His preoccupation with Indian music was clearly demonstrated by a piece he recorded titled "India." The musical compositions and improvisations of Ornette Coleman, John Coltrane, and Art Blakey can clearly demonstrate their interest in the music cultures of Tunisia, Morocco, and other predominantly Isla-

mic countries of the Near East and Africa.[9]

During the early twentieth century, Europeans in general, composers and painters in particular, were more receptive to African, African-derived, and Asian cultures than they had been earlier. That great representative of European music, composer Hector Berlioz, could say in 1862, for example, that "the Chinese sing like dogs howling, like a cat screeching when it has swallowed a toad"; European ignorance about non-European cultures was then truly appalling. But the years 1900 to 1913 brought such radical changes in attitude and new developments in musical creativity and scholarship that European and American composers, such as Claude Debussy, Igor Stravinsky, Arnold Schoeberg, Alan Berg, Anton Webern, Bela Bartok, Charles Ives, Olivier Messiaen, and Aaron Copland, to name a few, were heavily incorporating African, Afro-American, and Asian elements in their musical compositions.

Afro-American music in particular had a profound influence on the musical styles of the West, from folk to popular to art forms. Twentieth century composers were deeply impressed by the syncopated rhythms, breaks, improvisation, the diversity of tone colors, and the performance techniques employed by black American musicians. Debussy used elements from black American music in his "Golliwog's Cake Walk" (from the suite *Children's Corner*, 1908) and Stravinsky in his "Ragtime" (from *The Soldier's Tale*, 1918). The French composer Darius Milhaud used jazz elements in his ballet *The Creation of the World (La Creation du*

9. For a detailed account on John Coltrane, see Mark C. Gridley's *Jazz Styles*, pp. 226–241.

monde, 1923) and the American Aaron Copland in his *Piano Concerto* (1926). The well-known popular composer George Gershwin, for example, used jazz elements in his *Rhapsody in Blue* (1924) and the opera *Porgy and Bess* (1934).[10]

It is true that the communications explosion and rapid transportation have turned the world into a global village. The authentic traditions of a few societies have been completely wiped out by the impact of European technology as well as by the societies' own choice to blindly follow the footpaths of Europe and the United States in the name of "modernization." In spite of the great diversity of substyles that have emerged, the jazz tradition is alive and strong; its stability and relative resistance to change are at the core of its vitality. It has not only gained a highly respectable place on the concert stages in the world of music today, but its strong influence has become a threat to the survival of native music cultures in Africa and Asia. Even European and American folk, popular, and classical traditions, often taken for granted, have not been spared from the influences of Afro-American music. Jazz has also gained legitimacy as an art form. Many universities, both in the United States and abroad, offer degree programs and courses in jazz theory, history, and performance. To discuss even a few of the most important substyles and to name the great black jazz performers that made history since classic jazz is beyond the scope of this introductory book.

It is important, however, to mention that black women—such as Billie Holiday, Ella Fitzgerald, Sarah Vaughan, and

Figure 19.3. Sarah Vaughan. De Vine One Corp. Regency Artists, Ltd.

Betty Carter, to mention just four—still continue to play a prominent role in the advancement of jazz. Sarah Vaughan, one of the few artists who came out of the European-oriented big band era of the 1930s and 1940s, kept African-derived improvisational singing alive. A graduate of the Earl Hines big band, she was then the first singer to exploit the European vibrato and Afro-Americanize it with her wide vocal fluctuation. She is considered the leading jazz vocalist of the 1980s. Betty Carter, the youngest of the great jazz singers and a student of the Detroit Conservatory of Music, is also a product of the big band era. However, her use of falsetto, ornamental phrasing, rhythmic virtuosity, ability to improvise solo and to imitate the sound of musical instruments, and her large repertoire of songs and *scat* (vocable) techniques have won her a place as one of the best carriers of the vital jazz tradition. After all, vocal music was the foundation of instrumen-

[10]Roger Kamien, *Music: An Appreciation*, pp. 372–378.

153

tal jazz. This historic bond between singers and instrumentalists has remained
one of the most important characteristics of jazz.

History has repeatedly demonstrated that adoption of foreign cultural
characteristics—in music, language, religion, and so on—commonly takes place
because of war, colonialism, or slavery. It
was almost always the defeated and the
colonized who imitated and adopted the
ways of the victors. For example, many
African nations adopted European ways
duing the periods of colonialism. Despite
a current drift back toward traditional
values, the Chinese heritage has been
almost lost under communism. War con-
tacts exposed Japan, Korea, and Vietnam
to many elements of American culture,
including some of the worst. In the case

of black American culture, the most unusual trend took place. The world, con-
sciously and at a surprising rate, adopted
the culture of a minority in the United
States long considered inferior. In fact,
most of the world's youth have either
picked up black mannerisims or are still
attempting to act, sing, talk, and dance
like Afro-Americans. The Afro hair style,
black-inspired hand salutations, body
movements of disco and other dance
types, and vocal techniques of contemporary, popular, and folk music singers
provide us with excellent examples of
conscious adoption of many black American cultural traits. A powerful form of
black lifestyle was thus fashioned in the
United States, the influence of which has
strongly affected the music and other
cultural traditions of the world.

*Figure 19.4. Betty Carter. LilJay Productions.
American Federation of Musicians.*

Basic Terms

If you cannot identify the terms, titles, or names that follow, look back at the text, where they appear in italic type. Additional information about some of them may also by found by checking the index.

jazz
hot concept
"Buddy" Charles Bolden's Ragtime Band
ragging
riffs
Storyville jazz
Stephen Foster
"Old Black Joe"
"Old Folks at Home"

Original Dixieland Jazz Band
classic jazz
Louis Armstrong
John Coltrane
ragas
talas
Porgy and Bess
scat

Bibliography

BLESH, RUDI, *Shining Trumpets: A History of Jazz*. New York: Da Capo Press, 1958.

GRIDLEY, MARK C., *Jazz Styles*. Englewood Cliffs, New Jersey: Prentice-Hall, 1978.

KAMIEN, ROGER, *Music: An Appreciation*. New York: McGraw-Hill Book Co., 1976.

KAUFMAN, FREDERICK, and JOHN P. GUCKIN, *The African Roots of Jazz*. Sherman Oaks, California: Alfred Publishing Co., 1979.

KEBEDE, ASHENAFI, "African Music in the Western Hemisphere," *African Music*. Paris: UNESCO, 1972.

MERRIAM, ALAN P., and FRADLEY H. GARNER, "Jazz—The Word," *Ethnomusicology, 12 (3—1968):373–369.*

SOUTHERN, EILEEN, *The Music of Black Americans*. New York: W.W. Norton & Co., 1971.

TIRRO, FRANK, *Jazz: A History*. New York: W. W. Norton & Co., 1977.

WATERMAN, RICHARD A., "African Influence on American Negro Music," *Acculturation in the Americas*. Chicago: University of Chicago Press, 1952.

_____, "Hot Rhythm in Negro Music," *Journal of the American Musicological Society 1:24–37.*

Discography

The Louis Armstrong Story, Vol. 1. Columbia CL 851.

Ascension. Impulse 95.

Impressions. Impulse 42.

The Music of New Orleans—Music of the Streets. Recorded by Samuel B. Charters. Folkways Records FA 2461.

Shape of Jazz to Come. Atlantic 1317.

The Smithsonian Collection of Classic Jazz. (6 excellent records). The Smithsonian Associates, Washington, D.C. 20560.

Sonny Terry's Washboard Band. Folkways Records FA 2006.

Index

157